# THE MESOPOTAMIA MESS

## THE BRITISH INVASION OF IRAQ IN 1914

## THE LESSONS WE COULD HAVE - AND SHOULD HAVE - LEARNED

by Jack Bernstein, Author/Editor
Jenny Kao, Graphic Designer

# ABOUT THE AUTHOR/EDITOR

Jack Bernstein is the author of six popular sales/marketing books that are used in both the workplace and as college textbooks. The titles include:

Local Store Marketing for Restaurants

The Menu

The Guide to Selling Advertising Space

The Perfect Media Kit

TQS: Total Quality Sales

Resume Writing and Interview Skills for Salespeople

Jack Bernstein is also the President of a foreign language translation company and the Publisher of a series of bilingual K-8 math workbooks and bilingual GED test prep workbooks.

Published by
InterLingua Publishing
423 South Pacific Coast Highway, Suite 208
Redondo Beach, California U.S A.
http://www.TheMesopotamiaMess.com

For more information call InterLingua Publishing at
(310)792-3637 or e-mail: TheMesopotamiaMess@gmail.com

ISBN: 978-1-60299-017-3

# *Dedication*

To those who served in the name of freedom

# AUTHOR/EDITOR'S NOTE

My primary function in the creation of this book has been more of an editor, blending of the information from many sources into one readable text, and less as an author. That portion which I can claim to have written has primarily been creating bridges between the works of others and clarifying discrepancies between the available literature.

The book is a compilation of more than a dozen documents that were found in the digital libraries of the U.S. and British military, as well as in early twentieth century newspapers, books and periodicals. Most of the documents from the military were made available by the Combat Studies Institute and the major contributions to this work have been provided by: Matthew W. Williams, Department of Defense (THE BRITISH EXPERIENCE IN IRAQ FROM 1914-1926: WHAT WISDOM CAN THE UNITED STATES. DRAW FROM ITS EXPERIENCE?); Lieutenant Colonel James D. Scudieri, United States Army (IRAQ, 2003-4 AND MESOPOTAMIA, 1914-18: A COMPARATIVE ANALYSIS IN ENDS AND MEANS); PETER J. LAMBERT, MAJOR, United States Air Force (THE FORGOTTEN AIRWAR: AIRPOWER IN THE MESOPOTAMIAN CAMPAIGN); Robert D. Ramsey III (ADVICE FOR ADVISORS: SUGGESTIONS AND OBSERVATIONS FROM LAWRENCE TO THE PRESENT); Bud Bishop, United States Navy (OPERATIONAL ART: AN ANALYSIS OF BRITIAN'S SOUTHWEST ASIA CAMPAIGN IN WORLD WAR I; and, a number of British Military websites reflecting on World War I. Other significant contributors include: LETTERS FROM MESOPOTAMIA FROM CAPTAIN ROBERT PALMER, WHO WAS KILLED IN THE BATTLE OF UM EL HANNAH, JUNE 21, 1916; A BRIEF OUTLINE OF THE CAMPAIGN IN MESOPOTAMIA by Lt. Col. R. Evans, M.C.,P.S.C.; and, THE WAR IN THE CRADLE OF THE WORLD by Eleanor Franklin Egan.

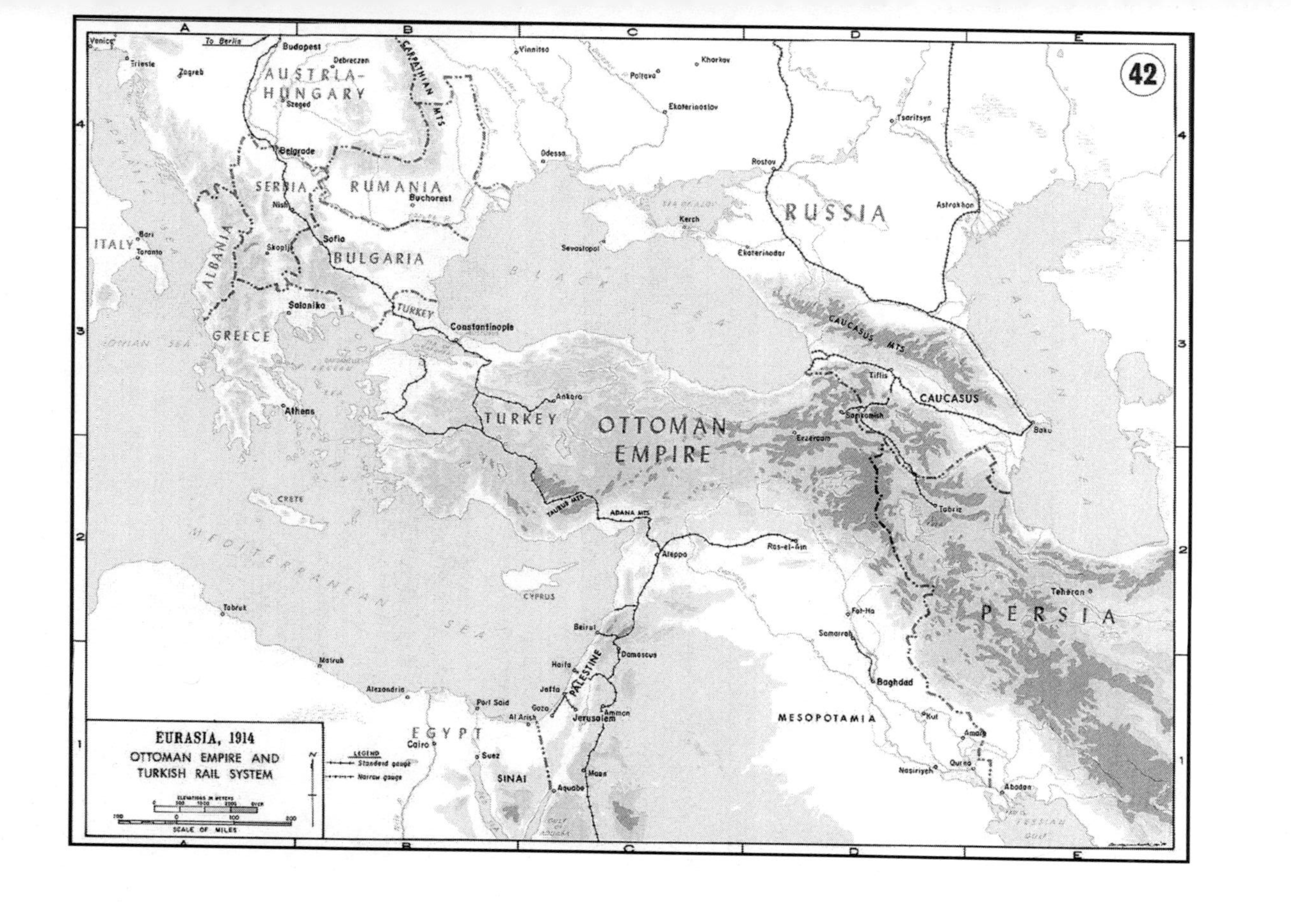
42
EURASIA, 1914
OTTOMAN EMPIRE AND
TURKISH RAIL SYSTEM
LEGEND
Standard gauge
Narrow gauge
ELEVATIONS IN METERS
SCALE OF MILES
AUSTRIA-HUNGARY
RUMANIA
SERBIA
BULGARIA
ALBANIA
GREECE
ITALY
TURKEY
OTTOMAN EMPIRE
RUSSIA
CAUCASUS
CAUCASUS MTS
CARPATHIAN MTS
TAURUS MTS
ADANA MTS
PERSIA
MESOPOTAMIA
PALESTINE
EGYPT
SINAI
CYPRUS
CRETE
BLACK SEA
MEDITERRANEAN SEA
To Berlin
Venice
Trieste
Zagreb
Budapest
Debreczen
Szeged
Belgrade
Nish
Bucharest
Sofia
Skoplje
Salonika
Athens
Bari
Taranto
Constantinople
Ankara
Vinnitsa
Odessa
Sevastopol
Poltava
Kharkov
Ekaterinoslav
Kerch
Ekaterinodar
Rostov
Tsaritsyn
Astrakhan
Tiflis
Sarikamish
Erzerum
Baku
Tabriz
Teheran
Aleppo
Ras-el-Ain
Beirut
Damascus
Haifa
Jaffa
Gaza
Jerusalem
Amman
Al Arish
Port Said
Alexandria
Cairo
Suez
Maan
Aquaba
Matruh
Tobruk
Fat-Ha
Samarra
Baghdad
Kut
Amara
Qurna
Nasiriyeh
Abadan

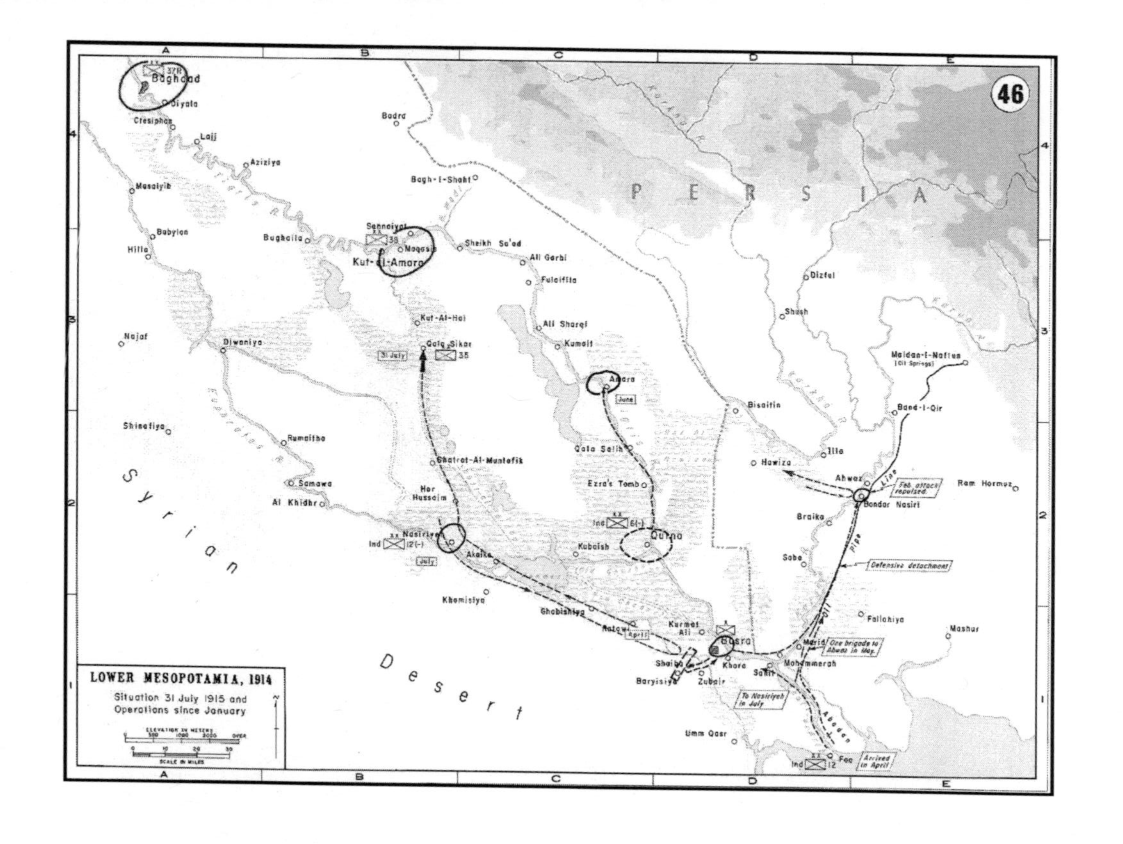
46
LOWER MESOPOTAMIA, 1914
Situation 31 July 1915 and
Operations since January
P E R S I A
Syrian Desert
Baghdad
Diyala
Ctesiphon
Lajj
Aziziya
Masaiyib
Babylon
Hilla
Najaf
Diwaniya
Shinafiya
Rumaitha
Samawa
Al Khidhr
Badra
Bagh-i-Shahi
Sennaiyat
Maqasis
Kut-al-Amara
Bughaila
Sheikh Sa'ad
Ali Garbi
Fulaifila
Ali Sharqi
Kumait
Amara
June
Kut-Al-Hai
Qala Sikar
31 July
Shatrat-Al-Muntafik
Hor Hussaim
Nasiriya
July
Akaika
Khamisiya
Ghabishiya
Ratawi
April
Kubaish
Qurna
Qala Salih
Ezra's Tomb
Kurmat Ali
Basra
Shaiba
Baryisiya
Zubair
Khora
Sahil
Umm Qasr
Mohammerah
Marid
One brigade to Ahwaz in May
To Nasiriyeh in July
Abadan
Fao
Arrived in April
Bisaitin
Hawiza
Illa
Ahwaz
Bandar Nasiri
Feb. attack repulsed
Braika
Saba
Defensive detachment
Fallahiya
Mashur
Ram Hormuz
Maidan-i-Naftun
(Oil Springs)
Band-i-Qir
Dizful
Shush
Oil Pipe Line
ELEVATION IN METERS
SCALE IN MILES

# TABLE OF CONTENTS

# INTRODUCTION

*In 1901 an Englishman, Mr. W. K. D'Arcy, obtained from H. R. H. the Shah a concession for working petroleum in all its forms in southern Persia. Mr. D'Arcy was "playing a lone hand." He was a courageous Englishman and he spent large sums of money in prospecting from one field to another, but without success. He exhausted his original capital and was then able to interest other capital in Burma and India as well as in England. In 1908, he discovered the long-sought-for area and tapped what proved to be an immense and practically inexhaustible oil-field. This field is in Arabistan, within the territories over which the Sheikh of Muhammerah exercises control.*

There are actually three stories in this book all woven into one. The first is of the British invasion, and the post invasion period.

In 1914, the British invaded Mesopotamia to protect their oil interests in the region. What began as a limited military initiative resulted in over four decades of active political and military involvement in that country.

In a hastily executed operation, without a real plan or objective, the British invaded Mesopotamia with a wholly inadequate and ill-prepared force, composed primarily of troops from India. There was absolutely no consideration given to the adverse weather conditions, non-existent infrastructure, requirements of keeping troops on the move supplied, civil administration, and so on. Despite all these adversities, they managed to defeat the troops of the Ottoman Empire in a war that lasted four years. After victory over the Turks, no consideration was made for the "post-invasion" period, and while the British controlled the government for decades and had to fight an insurgency that lasted for many years, they presented themselves to the local population as liberators.

The second story of this book is how similar the situation is between the British following its invasion in 1914 and the U.S. after its 2003 invasion. As soon as the hostilities ceased, wide scale looting occurred in both wars, and neither the British nor U.S. leaders appreciated the deep divide between the religious sects, nor their willingness to resort to violence to resolve their differences. Both governments expected that once the yoke of oppression was lifted from their shoulders, the people of Iraq would focus on building a future, and not settling old scores. Both the British and the U.S. shared a vision of the three communities of Iraq working together as a single nation, but found a dysfunctional civil administration and little interest in comingling of cultures under one rule. Both governments accepted their roles as keepers of the peace, protecting the people; but the local population only saw occupiers which they fought with bloody local insurgencies. Both the British and the U.S. expected more assistance from their allies than they received, and sadly, both were completely unprepared for the enormous fnancial investment that had to be made and the terrible cost in human lives resulting from their invasions.

There were many lessons that could have been – and should have been - learned from the British experience prior to the U.S. led invasion in 2003. What's sad is that a brief study of history could have anticipated, and avoided, many of the problems that have occurred. Unfortunately, this is war, and the consequences of ignoring history isn't an academic exercise, but rather, a human tragedy.

The third story of this book is how readily available the information about the British experience in Mesopotamia is to anyone who chooses to search for it. Most of the documents used in this book were readily available from the digital libraries of both the U.S. and British militaries, and that information was augmented by newspapers, magazines and books from that period. The book also includes some of the writings of Thomas Edward (T.E.) Lawrence, Lawrence of Arabia, which are well-known and readily available. He, more than anyone, understood the Arab culture and the problems of occupation, and offered many suggestions on how our nations and cultures could work and live together.

One would have hoped that the architects of the U.S. policy in Iraq would have spent a few hours on the internet researching the history of invasions into that region before launching one of our own.

# CHAPTER 1

# IT'S DÉJÀ VU, ALL OVER AGAIN

From: THE LONDON DAILY EXPRESS
December, 1922

MESOPOTAMIAN QUICKSAND.
—*The Daily Express* (London).

# CHAPTER 2

# A MESSAGE FROM LAWRENCE OF ARABIA ET. AL.

The following article about the British occupation of Iraq (Mesopotemia) was written by T.E. Lawrence, whose organization and direction of the Hedjaz against the Turks was one of the outstanding romances of World War I.

As background, it should be noted that during World War I, some Iraqis fought with Amir Feisal and the British to defeat Turkish forces because of a promise of a post-war independent Arab kingdom. After failing to deliver on that promise, the British quelled a significant uprising in 1920, and fought a low-level insurgency until 1931, when the British eventually handed over the majority of power to the Iraqis by establishing a pro-British monarchy in 1932.

Article From: THE SUNDAY TIMES
August 2nd, 1920

By T.E. Lawrence

The people of England have been led in Mesopotamia into a trap from which it will be hard to escape with dignity and honour. They have been tricked into it by a steady withholding of information. The Baghdad communiques are belated, insincere, incomplete. Things have been far worse than we have been told, our administration more bloody and inefficient than the public knows. It is a disgrace to our imperial record, and may soon be too inflamed for any ordinary cure. We are today not far from a disaster.

The sins of commission are those of the British civil authorities in Mesopotamia (especially of three 'colonels') who were given a free hand by London. They are controlled from no Department of State, but from the empty space which divides the Foreign Office from the India Office. They availed themselves of the necessary discretion of wartime to carry over their dangerous independence into times of peace. They contest every suggestion of real self-government sent them from home. A recent proclamation about autonomy circulated with unction from Baghdad was drafted and published out there in a hurry, to forestall a more liberal statement in preparation in London, 'Self-determination papers' favourable to England were extorted in Mesopotamia in 1919 by official pressure, by aeroplane demonstrations, by deportations to India.

The Cabinet cannot disclaim all responsibility. They receive little more news than the public: they should have insisted on more, and better. They have sent draft after draft of reinforcements, without enquiry. When conditions became too bad to endure longer, they decided to send out as High commissioner the original author of the present system, with a conciliatory message to the Arabs that his heart and policy have completely changed.*

Yet our published policy has not changed, and does not need changing. It is that there has been a deplorable contrast between our profession and our practice. We said we went to Mesopotamia to defeat Turkey. We said we stayed to deliver the Arabs from the oppression of the Turkish Government, and to make available for the world its resources of corn and oil. We spent nearly a million men and nearly a thousand million of money to these ends. This year we are spending ninety-two thousand men and fifty millions of money on the same objects.

Our government is worse than the old Turkish system. They kept fourteen thousand local conscripts embodied, and killed a yearly average of two hundred Arabs in maintaining peace. We keep ninety thousand men, with aeroplanes, armoured cars, gunboats, and armoured trains. We have killed about ten thousand Arabs in this rising this summer. We cannot hope to maintain such an average: it is a poor country, sparsely peopled; but Abd el Hamid would applaud his masters, if he saw us working. We are told the object of the rising was political, we are not told what the local people want. It may be what the Cabinet has promised them. A Minister in the House of Lords said that we must have so many troops because the local people will not enlist. On Friday the Government announced the death of some local levies defending their British officers, and say that the services of these men have not yet been sufficiently recognized because they are too few (adding the characteristic Baghdad touch that they are men of bad character). There are seven thousand of them, just half the old Turkish force of occupation. Properly officered and distributed, they would relieve half our army there. Cromer controlled Egypt's six million people with five thousand British troops; Colonel Wilson fails to control

Mesopotamia's three million people with ninety thousand troops.

We have not reached the limit of our military commitments. Four weeks ago the staff in Mesopotamia drew up a memorandum asking for four more divisions. I believe it was forwarded to the War Office, which has now sent three brigades from India. If the North-West Frontier cannot be further denuded, where is the balance to come from? Meanwhile, our unfortunate troops, Indian and British, under hard conditions of climate and supply, are policing an immense area, paying dearly every day in lives for the wilfully wrong policy of the civil administration in Baghdad. General Dyer was relieved of his command in India for a much smaller error, but the responsibility in this case is not on the Army, which has acted only at the request of the civil authorities. The War Office has made every effort to reduce our forces, but the decisions of the Cabinet have been against them.

The Government in Baghdad have been hanging Arabs in that town for political offences, which they call rebellion. The Arabs are not at war with us. Are these illegal executions to provoke the Arabs to reprisals on the three hundred British prisoners they hold? And, if so, is it that their punishment may be more severe, or is it to persuade our other troops to fight to the last?

We say we are in Mesopotamia to develop it for the benefit of the world. All experts say that the labour supply is the ruling factor in its development. How far will the killing of ten thousand villagers and townspeople this summer hinder the production of wheat, cotton, and oil? How long will we permit millions of pounds, thousands of Imperial troops, and tens of thousands of Arabs to be sacrificed on behalf of colonial administration which can benefit nobody but its administrators?

*Sir Percy Cox was to return as High Commissioner in October, 1920 to form a provisional Government.

Article From: THE LITERARY DIGEST
September 25, 1920

TROUBLESOME MESOPOTAMIA

MILITARY REINFORCEMENTS plus a high commissioner sent to Mesopotamia by the British Government must deal with "a critical situation" as the British press view it. News stories of the spread of "the war" feature besieged garrisons unrelieved; the killing or capture of British officers; communications and railways cut; the country around Baghdad dominated by insurgent tribal bands, and administrative officers driven from their posts in various districts. Press outcry against a drifting policy the London Mail expresses by saying, "The Government must make up its mind about Mesopotamia and stick to it. It must either go right in or come right out." Criticism of the War Office abounds for holding back news, for scattering units over a field infested with guerrilla tribesmen, for permitting the situation to get so out of hand that troops needed in India must be lifted for reinforcement. A Persian correspondent to The Times declared, "we are engaged in a war as expensive as and more exhausting than the South-African War." Among editorial exhortations to the Government in The Times we read:

"All the oil in Asia could not compensate us for the sacrifices we have made, the thousands of lives destroyed, and the hundreds of millions of pounds poured into that repellent region. The pretense that we are staying there for the good of the inhabitants is difficult to maintain. Unless there is a complete change of policy, Mesopotamia, which through the ages has been the grave of empires, is now likely to become the grave of the Coalition."

The appointment of Sir Percy Cox as high commissioner, however, is welcomed by The Times as evidence of changing policy. He belongs to the Indian Political Department, was political officer with the British forces in the Mesopotamian campaign that defeated the Turks in the Great War and initiated the temporary civil administration, was for years the principal British resident on the Persian Gulf, latterly serving as minister in Teheran, and he negotiated the Anglo-Persian Treaty. Semiofficial statements describe his mission as one of setting up "an independent state to be governed in accordance with the wishes of the people," conforming to the policy of the Anglo-French Declaration of November, 1918, in favor of "an independent Arab state by advice and assistance of a mandatory Power." The further semiofficial statement that military administration was never intended to be the permanent form of Mesopotamian administration, according to The Times, has been belied by the acts done. "If any one can form an Arab administration out of very unpromising material," Sir Percy Cox will do so, that paper declares, but first of all military occupation must cease at the earliest possible moment.

Colonel T. E. Lawrence, famous as leader of the Arab war on the Turks, however, is by no means satisfied: "The system represented by Sir Percy Cox will not square up; the people of England have been led into a trap from which it will be hard to escape with dignity and honor." He writes in The Sunday Times:

"When conditions became too bad to endure longer, the Cabinet decided to send out as high commissioner the original author of the present system, with a conciliatory message to the Arabs that his heart and policy have completely changed.

"Yet our published policy has not changed, and does not need changing. It is that there has been a deplorable contrast between our profession and our practice. We said we went to Mesopotamia to defeat Turkey. We said we stayed to deliver the Arabs from the oppression of the Turkish Government, and to make available for the world its resources of corn and oil. We spent nearly a million men and nearly a thousand million of money to these ends. This year we are spending ninety-two thousand men and fifty millions of money on the same objects. We say we are in Mesopotamia to develop it for the benefit of the world. All experts say that the labor supply is the ruling factor in its development. How far will the killing of ten thousand villagers and townspeople this summer hinder the production of wheat, cotton, and oil? How long will we permit millions of pounds, thousands of imperial troops, and tens of thousands of Arabs to be sacrificed on behalf of a form of colonial administration which can benefit nobody but its administrators?

The "tragedy of Mesopotamia" is that "the poison" of the Indian Government officialdom came in after the death of Sir Stanley Maude, who took Baghdad in 1917, and gradually won the enthusiastic support of the somewhat reserved Arabs, according to "one of Maude's officers," in the Manchester Guardian. This writer declares that the Arab follower of

Mohammed will not tolerate the Hindu, whom he considers an inferior race. It is "hopeless folly" — now to be reinforced — to garrison the country with Indian troops. The Indian official "has no more qualification for governing the Arab than has the Eskimo for governing the Chinese. The direction of Mesopotamian affairs must be taken from India and placed in the hands of the home government. The Arabs must, have a full share in working out their own salvation."

The situation is made doubly difficult by the divison between British and French policy, observes the Manchester Guardian:

"The vision of a homogeneous Arab state, fostered by French influence in the north and by British in the south, becomes less likely of realization. Following the deposition of Emir Faysal by the French comes the appointment of his brother by the British Government to rule in their sphere of influence. Faysal himself is on his way to Europe, all will doubtless seize on the rift in Allied diplomacy to appeal to British sympathies. Meanwhile, so long has a firm and wise Allied policy for the whole region between the Mediterranean and the Persian Gulf been delayed that the actual warfare which the French have brought on themselves in the north has its counterpart in continued and often serious guerilla fighting in the British zones. An attempt to fulfill the pledges of the Peace Treaty is being conscientiously but tardily made by Britain in the calling together of a national assembly at Bagdad."

Since the Government has neither the money nor men demanded for continued prosecution of "these distant and doubtful ventures," the London Daily News favors restricted occupation, saying:

"The southern part of the Basra vilayet — the line Nasiriya-Kurnah would be an obvious frontier, leaving the tribesmen of Bagda and Mosul to live their habitual life - under our nominal suzerainty exercised under mandate. That might mean some loss of prestige. But at the present rate there will soon be little of it to lose."

But the London Chronicle repeats advice "to keep cool heads about Mesopotamia," while "attempts are being made in the usual quarters to work up an anti-governmental scare." Why should Great Britain render policing service to civilized natives against lawless tribesmen? To quote The Chronicle:

"A popular answer in some quarters is 'oil'; but it is one which can only be made in gross ignorance of in bad faith. The British Empire's interest in the region existed long before oil was thought of, and would exist if no oil were there. The 'jugular artery' of the Empire is the Suez Canal and Red Sea; and the further passage to India is dominated by the Persian Gulf. The Middle East countries dominating these seaboards — Palestine, Arabia, Mesopotamia, Persia — are countries which we have never tried to rule in the past, but which it has always been important for us to prevent from falling under the domination of a Great Power hostile to ourselves.

"Our aim must still be not to annex these countries, but to foster local free states in them. In Persia, we have been and are practically the sole factor, which keeps an independent state alive. In Palestine, we hope to develop a free Jewish state. In the greater part of Arabia, we look to King Hussein and the Emir Faysal. It has been suggested that we should hand Mesopotamia over to Faysal. It might be a good solution, if he is equal to the task; but that condition needs to be very carefully examined. Failing him, there is no visible alternative but to undertake it ourselves, under the international mandate conferred either on us, or to leave it open for future aggression by others. This last course may appear cheap and easy at the moment; but if we are really anxious 'to avoid future wars' — real wars, not local operations like those now in progress — we shall not take it."

Article From: THE LONDON TIMES
Tuesday, June 15.

A CASE FOR FRANKNESS

The questions which LORD ISLINGTON proposed to address to the Government today in the House of Lords upon Mesopotamia have been postponed for a week. We do not regret the delay, for the questions did not go nearly far enough. We shall have to probe much more deeply before we learn the whole truth about the Government's mysterious, costly, and questionable policy in the Middle East. LORD ISLINGTON intended to ask what form of civil administration will be set up in Mesopotamia; the number of officers now engaged in civil administration and the number of troops stationed there; the cost to the British taxpayer of our present occupation of the country; and under which Department of the Government the country "is now being and will be administered".

We doubt whether any questions will elicit all the information required, because the Government's statements upon Mesopotamia have long been vitiated by evasions, concealments, and half-truths; but, in any case, Lord Islington questions should be framed upon a wider basis. The Government's policy in Mesopotamia, and the money they are freely spending there, cannot be dissociated from the question of Persia because policy and expenditure in both countries are inextricably interwoven. The general who commands in Mesopotamia " commands," too, in North-West Persia. There is also General Malleson, who "commands" at Meshed, in North-Eastern Persia, and whose force has long cost large sums for a purpose, which we fail to comprehend. Again, Lord Islington must be sufficiently familiar with Oriental methods to know that in these countries the number of troops is only one element in the question. Has he forgotten the "followers"? He should inquire how many people are on the "ration strength." It is said that there are 200,000 "followers" in Mesopotamia alone; and we believe it will be found that, counting "followers" the British taxpayer is paying for nearly 400,000 people in these two countries. It must further be pointed out that inquiries about Mesopotamia, which omit any reference to oil, are almost futile. The Government ought frankly to say how far the War Office has been dabbling in the question of oil concessions, and should state quite clearly what promises have been made to various oil interests behind the back of Parliament.

If, a week hence, the Government tells the truth, they will admit that, despite their solemn undertaking just after Turkey surrendered, they have been breaking their pledge "to allow the people of Mesopotamia to choose their own form of government. They have given the head of the local civil administration, Colonel Wilson, so much uncontrolled power that he has attempted to "Indianize" Mesopotamia, apparently without much regard to his superiors. Colonel Wilson, who seems to combine inexhaustible energy with a dangerous tendency to disregard the broader aspects of Imperial policy, has acted as though Great Britain proposes to take permanent possession of Mesopotamia and to keep it under direct British rule. The frequent outbreaks in these areas are to some extent, a consequence of his excessive activities. Had we left the people of both Southern and Northern Kurdistan to manage their own affairs, we should probably have had none of the expensive "punitive" expeditions of the last twelve months. It does not gladden our hearts to learn that after the deplorable assassinations of British officers and armoured-car crews at Tel Afar, a number of Arabs have been killed by way of retaliation.

If we had kept our pledges of November, 1918, renewed in the Turkish Peace Treaty, these regrettable affrays might never have occurred. As to the oil question, we trust the Government will give some explanation in regard to the presence, or the recent presence, of General Sir John Cowans in Mesopotamia. It is understood that Sir John Cowans is the representative, at a very large salary, of certain oil interests.

On his retirement from the Army he had every right to follow what occupation he pleased; but, at a time when the War Office was still responsible for the control of Mesopotamia, we should have preferred to have seen oil interests represented in that region by another man than by the distinguished officer who, so recently as last year, was Quartermaster-General of the Forces and a member of the Army Council. We take it for granted that, in his capacity as an oil representative, Sir John Cowans did not journey through Mesopotamia "in full regimentals," as has been publicly alleged. An uncomfortable feeling prevails that various Government Departments have been making promises to oil interests—and to other interests — which may incidentally involve the country in heavy responsibilities and untold expenditure. Only yesterday it was stated in various newspapers that a British firm was about to acquire a great carpet factory at Tabriz, in Persia, and that "the Foreign Office has promised constant "State protection." Such a statement is incredible. The small detachment of British troops recently stationed in Tabriz was known to be in a position of considerable danger, and there is no place in the Middle East where we are less able to afford "constant State protection" then the capital of Persian - Azerbaijan.

We trust that Ministers will state frankly what promises they have made. We trust also that the Government will lose no time in framing and in announcing — preferably in agreement with France — a sound and intelligible policy in regard to the idle East.

# CHAPTER 3

# IN THE BEGINNING

Iraq. It seems like the center of the known universe. Not a newspaper, not a TV station, not a politician, fails to mention it several times a day, everyday. At one time *it was* the known universe. Mesopotamia, as the area was originally known, is purported to be the site of the biblical Garden of Eden and the first civilized societies truly sprang from there. The ancient Sumerians, the people of the Tigris and Euphrates river basin, developed complex irrigation systems, which resulted in the first cereal agriculture, allowing for the production of surplus food and the molding of a civilized society. They're responsible for developing what is probably the world's earliest writing system, known as cuneiform, and their successors, the Akkadians, devised the most complete legal system of the period, the Code of Hammurabi.

Civilization flourished in Mesopotamia, or the "land between the rivers," because the annual flooding gave the plains a natural fertility, and in the lower regions there were significant areas of permanent marshland. But the rivers created more than just a viable agricultural economy; because they were navigable, they gave the people access to the rest of the world. The Tigris flows from the Turkish border through Baghdad and Kut, and the Euphrates flows from the Syrian border through Fallujah and Najaf. The two rivers meet at Qurna to form the Shatt-al-Arab for the last hundred miles past Basra to the Persian Gulf at Fao.

Over the centuries Mesopotamia was conquered by Darius, Alexander, Rome, and most importantly, Islam.

In 637, an Arab army defeated the then ruling Persians near the present-day city of Qadisiyyah - a victory of great symbolic importance to Iraqis today. This battle led to the fall of the capital of the Persian Sassanids at Ctesiphon and the expansion of an Arab Empire led by Umar ibn Al-Khattab, the second caliph. Islamic in character, Umar primarily conquered new lands both to secure the unity of the ummah (Muslim community) and to enrich his treasury. However, he did not force non-Muslim subjects to convert to Islam.[2] Umar subsequently built two garrison towns, or amsar, in Iraq at Al-Kufah and Basra, where Islamic soldiers were purposely segregated from their conquered populations.

Uthman ibn Affan succeeded Umar and became the third caliph in 644. He was a member of the powerful Umayyad family whose descendents ultimately ruled this Islamic Empire until 750. Mutinous Arab soldiers murdered Uthman in 656 because of his alleged nepotism and failure to provide the benefits that the soldiers thought they deserved. These mutineers claimed Ali ibn Abi Talib, son-in-law to the Prophet, as their new caliph thanks to his family ties to Muhammed and his prior opposition to Uthman and Umar.

Ali subsequently led a civil war against Umayyad loyalists and made Al-Kufah his capital. Marching his army on Basra from Al-Kufah, he defeated opposition forces at the Battle of the Camel in 656. Muawiya, a powerful member of the Umayyad located in Damascus, Syria was Ali's primary nemesis, and the armies of the two leaders fought in Damascus in 657. The fierce battle ultimately ended in a truce, as both sides agreed to arbitrate the secession according to the Quran. Arbitration took place six months later but proved inconclusive.[3]

In 658, Muawiya annexed Egypt and proclaimed himself caliph in Jerusalem, splitting the Islamic Empire. Muawiya ruled Syria, Egypt, and Palestine while Ali controlled Iraq and Persia. Frustrated at this division and convinced that only the assassination of both leaders would reunite all Muslims, a group of Kharijites (who believed that the caliph should be the most committed Muslim, not the most politically powerful) tried to kill Muawiya and Ali in 661. Muawiya survived the assassination attempt but Ali was struck down outside his mosque in Al-Kufah.[4]

Undeterred, some of Ali's supporters proclaimed his son, Hasan, as the new caliph. But Hasan, the grandson of the Prophet, had no interests in continuing the bloody struggle of his father since he considered this struggle contrary to Muhammed's message, and agreed with Muawiya to retire to Medina. When he died in 669, Muawiya became the next caliphate and ruled from 661-80. He reunited the Islamic Empire, captured Rhodes, expanded territory in North Africa, raided Sicily, and unsuccessfully besieged Constantinople.

Muawaiya died in 680. Prior to his death, he appointed his son, Yazid I, as the next caliph. Dissatisfied with this succession, Ali's former followers called on Husein, Ali's other son, to assume the caliphate. Heeding this call and refusing to submit to Yazid's authority, Husein marched to Iraq to consolidate his support. Soldiers loyal to Yazid and the Umayyad family surrounded Husein and killed him outside of Karbala, Iraq in 680.[5] This event represented the second time that one of the Prophet's direct descendants had been killed in Iraq. Ali and Husein, both martyrs of Shia Islam, were buried in al Najaf and Karbala, respectively.

The Abbasid faction, claiming to be descended from the Prophet's Uncle Abbas and his son Abdallah, overthrew the Umayyad dynasty in 750. In the period of the Abbasid caliphs (750-1258), Iraq was the center of a huge Islamic empire stretching from the plains of India in the east to present day Morocco. Abbasid Caliph Abu Jafar al-Mansur laid the foundations of his capital approximately sixty miles from the ancient city of Babylon and named it Baghdad. Baghdad eventually became a worldwide center of medicine, science, philosophy, law, art and trade, with lands as far away as Africa, Asia, and the Far East.

As Eleanor Franklin Egan, a British journalist, explained in 1918:

> Mesopotamia is inhabited solely by Arab tribes, and the Arabs are all Mohammedans. But the Mohammedans of the world are divided into two main sects by irreconcilable differences of religious opinion; sects which in Mesopotamia have indulged in innumerable fearful contests for supremacy, all of which have tended to sink the country further and further into moral ruin and material exhaustion.

The two great Mohammedan sects are the Sunnis and the Shiahs. The Sunnis acknowledge the succession of the first four Khaliphs and the right of the Sultan of Turkey to the spiritual and temporal predominance bequeathed by the Prophet, and the greatest tribe of Sunni Arabs in Mesopotamia and eastern Arabia the Muntafik joined the Turks at the beginning of the war and have succeeded, by frequent raids and constant guerrilla warfare, in making things very unpleasant at times for the British on the River Euphrates.

But the Shiahs deny the succession of the first four Khaliphs and recognize as the true heir of the Prophet the Imam Ali, who married Mohammed's daughter Fatima. The sons of Fatima, Al-Hasan and Al-Husein, rebelled against the Khaliphate and, according to Shiah belief, were treacherously slain. They became the martyrs of the Shiah sect and the anniversary of their death became the principle Shiah Mohammedan holy day. It is celebrated throughout the Shiah world which, includes a large part of Mohammedan India, with processions of mourning and, in some localities, with a frenzied fanaticism which expresses itself in self-flagellation and other forms of self-torture, and in murderous attacks on men of other faiths. The Shiahs, of course, do not acknowledge the Sultan of Turkey. Rather they abhor what they regard as his usurpation of a holy office. And a fact which relieves the British situation of at least one complication is that a majority of the Arabs

> behind the British lines in Mesopotamia are Shiahs.
>
> The holy cities of the Sunnis are Mecca and Medina in western Arabia, while the chief places of devout pilgrimage for the Shiahs are Kerbela and Nejef, west of the Euphrates in Mesopotamia. Kerbela contains the tomb of the martyr Husein, while the sacred shrine of Ali is at Nejef. And these two towns are now in the hands of the British, who are adept from long practice in the gentle art of respecting other peoples' beliefs.[1]

At the beginning of the thirteenth century, after a long history of conquest and counter conquest, Mesopotamia was a fertile, flourishing and civilized country; then came the Mongol invasion, when the savage hordes of Jenghis Khan and, later, Hulaku Khan poured down out of the north upon Persia and Armenia, sweeping everything before them by the bitterness and violence of their animosity against Islam. In 1258 A.D. the invaders reached Baghdad. The capital was sacked, and the scientific, literary, and artistic records of centuries were wiped out; the system of irrigation, upon which the country depended for its existence, was destroyed; and, after a period of civilization which had lasted for eight centuries, Mesopotamia once more lay wasted, an arid desert save for the two great rivers which wound their way, past a few scattered vestiges of humanity, towards the Persian Gulf.[1.1]

In 1509, the Persian Safavid Empire expanded its territory and incorporated most of present day Iraq. Control of Iraq changed hands periodically between the Safavid Empire and the

Ottoman Empire for the next 100 years. In 1638, the Ottoman Sultan, Murad IV, expelled the Persians and initiated a period of uninterrupted Ottoman rule until World War I. Iraq benefited from the Ottoman Tanzimat era of the 1860s - a period of administration, conscription, law, and public education reforms which included the establishment of private property. These reforms replaced the feudal system of land ownership and tax farms with legally sanctioned property rights.

At this time, the traders of the West were endeavoring to exploit the commercial possibilities of the East, and the trade routes into Persia from the south and west ran through Baghdad. British commerce was so largely engaged in commerce in the region that in the eighteenth century England undertook the responsibility for the protection of shipping from the pirates, which then infested the Persian Gulf and the Shatt-al-Arab.

The Turks administered Iraq as three separate provinces or vilayets (Mosul, Baghdad, and Basra) under appointed Ottoman governors. This administration was structured on the country's ethnic makeup. Generally speaking, Iraq was populated by Kurds in the north (along with Christian Chaldeans and Assyrians), Sunnis in the central part of the country, and Shias in the south. Overall, the Ottoman administration focused on the Tigris and Euphrates valleys, where the majority of the population lived. During this period, the Sunnis gained the administrative experience that has allowed them to monopolize political power in the twentieth century, and they were able to take advantage of new educational and economic opportunities. On the other hand, the Shias were removed from the political process, and subsequently, were impoverished. Binary politics became the basis for internal conflict in Iraq for many generations to come.

The British put an end to the Ottoman administration in World War I. As Eleanor Franklin Egan reports:

> British "occupation" of lower Mesopotamia and the country immediately round the Persian Gulf antedates the war by several centuries, and the story of it begins with the dislodgment of the Portuguese from the now deserted island of Hormuz. The British East India Company had reached a trade agreement with the Shah of Persia, and the Portuguese sought to interfere with the legitimate advance of British interests.
>
> Those were the days of uncharted seas and of merchant adventurers who sailed them in search of adventure. For generations the favorite occupations of the coast Arabs in these regions have been piracy, slave trading, and gun-running. And it must be taken into consideration that Turkey's notoriety for iniquitous governmental methods is no new thing and that Turkish overlordship in the Arabian peninsula has never been a success. It has never been a success up along the Tigris and Euphrates, either, but in those regions there has been some semblance of control. At Basra and at points above, there have always been Turkish pashas representing the Sublime Porte as resident governors, and they have been backed by military garrisons.

Below Basra there are two great divisions of the Arab peoples. They are themselves divided into many tribes and tribal groups, but are allied in strong confederations on the Mesopotamian side of the gulf to resist Turkish aggression, and on the Persian side to resist Persian interference with ancient rights and liberties and they have never acknowledged any authority except that of their own sheikhs.

The two most important of these Arab chieftains are the Sheikh of Kuweit and the Sheikh of Muhammerah, and if these two had not been lifelong friends of Britain, upholding a traditional friendship of their fathers before them, the occupation of Mesopotamia by British troops would have been much more difficult.

The principality of the Sheikh of Kuweit extending one hundred and sixty miles in one direction and one hundred and ninety miles in another lies on the Mesopotamian side of the upper gulf and has been ruled by the family of the patriarchal old Jabir-ibn-Mubarak, who rules it now, since the middle of the seventeenth century.

The territories of the Sheikh of Muhammerah are in Persian Arabistan, just across on the other side, and together these two picturesque rulers can provide a force of fifty-odd thousand men armed with good serviceable rifles. They have provided no force to support the British, but they easily could have provided such a force to oppose them had they been persuaded to ally themselves with the Turks.

But it is due almost entirely to England's friendly assistance in the past that these sheikhs are what they are and that they are able to exercise even a partial control over their numerous and turbulent tribes.

It was to the interest of everybody economically concerned in the regions round about, and especially of the Sheikh of Kuweit, that piracy should be suppressed in the Persian Gulf. Pearling is one of the chief pursuits of the coast Arabs there being the two wonderful little islands of Bahrein and Mubarak just south of Kuweit, the pearl fisheries of which have netted their owners in a good year as much as half a million pounds sterling and in the pearling season, particularly, the upper gulf has always been a pirates' paradise.

Turkey could not patrol these waters, though, considering her claim to sovereignty over them, it was her business to do so. The Arab sheikhs had no naval vessels of any kind, and Persia was helpless. It therefore fell to the lot of England to police the gulf, just as it has fallen to the lot of England to police nearly all the otherwise unpoliced waters of the earth.

From the beginning British influence rapidly increased, this being due not so much to the greater energy and enterprise of the English traders as to the fact that England was willing to undertake the establishment and maintenance of peaceful conditions

> in the ports and the safeguarding of navigation in the gulf. English influence with the Mesopotamian peoples has been the result of nothing but the honorable and generally satisfactory discharge on England's part of tremendous responsibilities.
>
> During the whole of the nineteenth century the British army and navy were used unsparingly in a never-ending effort to suppress the notorious slave trade with the east coast of Africa. But it is a notable fact that before mere British supremacy of influence gave way in 1914 to absolute British control in the gulf, the iniquitous traffic in human beings was by no means extinct. And to realize the extent of slavery in all parts of Arabia, Mesopotamia, and Persia one has only to observe the evidence of African blood in vast numbers of the people and the presence among the tribes of innumerable black human beasts of burden.

In addition to trade, the British sought the prevention of any other European power, in particular Russia, from establishing its influence in the region. Britain suspected that an expansionist-minded, tsarist-ruled Russia intended to impose a protectorate over Persia in order to secure an ice-free port in the Persian Gulf. Since this potentially threatened British interests in India, the British directed significant diplomatic efforts to thwart Russian influence in the area.[6]

Ironically, during World War I, Russia was an important ally of Britain, but in the decades prior to World War I, Britain strongly supported Turkey against Russia, especially during the Russo-Turkish War of 1878.

# CHAPTER 4

# THE POLITICS BEHIND THE WAR

The relationship between the Ottoman Empire and Germany began during Chancellor Bismarck's administration. In the mid-1880s, the Chancellor dispatched civil and military advisors to assist the Empire's attempts to modernize along European lines, and German businesses exploited this new relationship to take advantage of new markets and raw materials on the Empire's eastern frontiers. The Chancellor sought to conduct this assistance discreetly so as not to provoke both Russia and Britain since they considered the Empire to be within their spheres of influence.

Kaiser Wilhelm II assumed power in the summer 1888 and subsequently pursued a more proactive relationship with the Empire. Even after the notorious Ottoman massacre of tens of thousands of Armenians (1894-1896), which isolated Constantinople from the rest of the world, Wilhelm II continued to develop relations with the Empire. In a widely publicized affair in late 1898, he visited Constantinople, Syria and Jerusalem, and in a speech in Damascus, he proclaimed himself the "Defender of Islam," protecting over 300 million Muslims living under British and Russian rule in Afghanistan, India, and central Russia.[7] Needless to say, this proclamation caused considerable consternation for British authorities in India, who were already delicately balancing the significant race and religious issues on the subcontinent.

To enhance German interests in the Empire, Wilhelm II subsequently authorized the construction of a railroad from Berlin to Basra via Baghdad. The railroad's "aim, both commercial and strategic, was to provide a shortcut to India and the East by bypassing the Suez Canal, which could be closed to shipping in the event of war."[8] The railway not only eliminated the British Royal Navy as a potential menace to German commerce in the Mediterranean, but it also posed a threat to Britain's line of communication to India.

In 1903, the German government attempted to get a concession for a railway terminus at Kuwait, and the Turkish government was bringing pressure to bear upon the independent sheikh to induce him to accept Turkish nationality and title along with Turkish sovereignty over his ancient hereditary domain. The Sheikh obstinately refused to both demands, so in the face of a Turkish ultimatum he appealed to the British for their assistance.

Since Britain viewed the potential of the railway and control of the area by the Germans and the Ottomans with alarm, they formulated a deal with the Sheikh of Kuwait that would ensure their continued access to the head of the Persian Gulf. The Sheikh promised not to cede any of his territory to any foreign power, and in return the British government promised to protect the Sheikh's throne and guarantee his territorial sovereignty.

The British senior naval officer in the gulf fleet drew up a plan for defense of Kuwait and landed some guns and marines to augment the forces of the Sheikh. But the Turks, not being prepared for anything so internationally serious, drew back, and the incident was closed. Though, as a result of the incident, it strengthened the bond between Britain and the Arab rulers, and established a recognized status for everybody concerned.

German assistance to the Empire increased significantly prior to World War I, including dispatching General Otto Liman von Sanders to act as a senior advisor to the Ottoman military. By the summer of 1914, Liman von Sanders led the German Military Mission, which consisted of thirty officers and forty enlisted soldiers. The Germans placed advisors throughout the Turkish Army's line units, training schools, and staff colleges.[9] Although Wilhelm II intended Liman von Sanders to take over the Ottoman military once hostilities started with the Entente (Britain, Russia and France, initially, then Italy and the United States joining later), the Turks relegated him to an advisory position only. Overall, the Germans had two goals for the Empire during the war: (1) sever communications (via the Bosphorus) between Russia and her Entente allies, and (2) ignite a pan-Islamic movement among the Muslim populations in British held territory to force Britain to divert troops away from the critical Western Front. The Germans and Turks expended considerable effort in encouraging Muslim disaffection, including spreading rumors that the Kaiser was a descendent of Muhammed's sister and had converted to Islam.

Despite European assistance to aid its internal reform, the Ottoman Empire had been steadily declining since the eighteenth century because of: internal corruption; inability to modernize; disastrous wars against Russia, Italy, and the Balkan nations; and inefficient management of colonial possessions. Britain, in fear that instability in Egypt threatened its access to the Suez Canal and its lines of communication to India, seized Ottoman-controlled Egypt in 1882, following anti-European riots led by nationalist elements.

The Empire also lost nearly all of its European territory in the First Balkan War of 1912, and as a result, its borders were more exposed to Greece and Bulgaria. Most of all, it was more vulnerable to Russia, its most bellicose neighbor in the East during the nineteenth century. Russia had armies in northern Persia and the Empire suspected it had designs on the Bosphorus Straits and even Constantinople itself.

All in all, prior to World War I, the Empire was weakened both politically and militarily, its borders had contracted, and its leadership suspected that the countries of the Entente had intentions of acquiring more of its territory.

On the eve of World War I, the Ottoman Empire was a constitutional monarchy led by a Sultan-Caliph and an elected parliament. In 1908, when Enver Pasha and the "Young Turks" overthrew the then existing regime and set up the Committee of Union and Progress (CUP) under which Turkish policy became markedly anti-British and aimed at the destruction of British prestige in Mohammedan eyes.

An inner circle of six Committee of Union and Progress members held the majority of power in the country and the officer corps, civil officials, and key provincial businessmen and politicians constituted their power base. This small inner circle consisted of Talat Bey, Interior Minister, who had considerable power due to his influence within the party; Halil Bey, leader of the lower house of parliament, Cavid Bey, the Finance Minister; Cemal Bey, Minister of the Navy; Enver Pasha, Minister of War; and Said Halim Pasha, the Grand Vizier and Foreign Minister who wielded less influence and power than his formal titles suggest. Prior to their entrance into the war, this inner circle was split on whether to go to war and on whose side they should choose. Said Halim and Cavid mostly favored neutrality while Enver and Talat promoted intervention on Germany's side, the only major European power that offered to protect the Empire from Russia. Enver chiefly favored intervention on the assumption of a short war.[10] While there was question as to which side the Ottomans would take in the war, in the end, the German supply of ships, money, and munitions helped propel the Empire on the side of the Central Powers. Enver thought the Empire could survive a short war with the majority of its territory left intact.[11]

The Empire's alliance with the Central Powers forced the British to better protect previously less defended areas that had strategic significance. The Suez Canal in Egypt and its oil facilities in southern Iraq were especially vulnerable to Turkish attack due to the lack of permanently based British troops.

Britain's reliance on strategic resources from the Persian Gulf began when oil was discovered in southwest Persia in 1908. As a consequence, the Anglo-Persian Oil Company was established in 1909 to exploit this discovery. The company built a pipe-line through the territory of the Sheikh of Mohammera, a semi-independent ruler, from Shustar to the island of Abadan in the Shatt-al-Arab, Iraq's only waterway access to the Persian

Gulf. The sheik, who for years had bitterly resented and resisted Turkish aggression, had contracted mutual obligations with the British for the protection of the pipe-line. Similar obligations had been concluded between the British and the Bakhtiari Khans, the chiefs of a group of tribes in the oilfields area.

In 1912, the importance of Persian oil became even more significant when the Royal Navy switched from coal to oil as its primary source of fuel, so in 1914 the British Admiralty bought a controlling interest in the enterprise by purchasing £2,200,000 worth of Ordinary Shares. While Britain's ability to defend its own territory and its overseas possessions depended on its unfettered access to Persian Gulf produced oil, it's interesting to note that Admiralty's investment was roundly criticized at the time for this seemingly unjustifiable extravagance.

In short, maintaining British prestige at the head of the Persian Gulf and in Persia was a leading principle in British policy in the Middle East in the years immediately preceding 1914. Britain had considerable economic access rights in the Basra vilayet including Anglo-Persian Oil Company's wells at Shustar; the hundred and forty miles of pipe-line which connected them with the refineries, and the refineries themselves, on the island of Abadan, at the mouth of the Shatt-al-Arab. Additionally, Britain had significant navigation rights on the Tigris and Euphrates rivers, and until 1914, British warships even had access to the Shatt-al-Arab. However, war with the Central Powers threatened that access and potentially put its lines of communication to India in peril. Similarly, British officials also feared a war with the Ottoman Empire could potentially foment both anti-British propaganda in Iraq, Persia, Afghanistan and the Muslim populated areas of India, and even an insurrection of the tribes located on the northwestern frontier between Afghanistan and India.

# CHAPTER 5

# THE BATTLE LINES ARE DRAWN

Unlike most of its European neighbors prior to World War I, Britain had a relatively limited army. Economic restraints and reforms carried out after the Boer War in South Africa (1899-1902) helped shape the British Army into a small, but highly trained force. In 1907, the British signed the Anglo-Russian Agreement and this entirely altered the political and military landscapes. With the Russian menace gone, and with Afghanistan friendly as it then was, the military horizon in India seemed clear, and reforms to upgrade the military put in place by Lord Kitchener, Commander-in-Chief, were abandoned for economic reasons. The Finance Member of the Viceroy's Council was so concerned about expenditures that they actually requested half-a-million pounds less for the Army in India in 1915-16, than in the previous year, when the war first broke out.

Ten days after the outbreak of hostilities in August 1914, Britain sent only four divisions to the Western Front in France.[12] Germany, in comparison, deployed seventy-three divisions against the Allies at the beginning of the war.[13] Since it viewed the Western Front as its primary theatre of operations during the war, Britain did not have the will to deploy a significant number of troops outside of the European continent. Therefore, it fell upon India to secure the borders of its own territory and to dispatch multiple expeditionary forces to fight in Europe, Africa, and Iraq.

The British Army in India was not designed or equipped to fight overseas. The "Army in India" Committee in 1912 submitted a "Majority Report" that stated the Army in India should only have three responsibilities: provide internal security, maintain India's territorial sovereignty, and be able to defend against a great power (e.g., Russia) until reinforced by Britain. However, this report also recommended that forces of the Army in India should be organized and equipped to accommodate deployment outside of India if required.[14]

Thus, in 1914, the Army in India took to the field deficient in artillery, ammunition, small arms, clothing, boots and equipment, modern machine-guns, signaling equipment, wire-cutters, grenades, and flares. (In these respects, indeed, the Turks, under German organization, were better equipped). The Army had only four modern aircraft, no wireless communications equipment, and it neither had reserve forces with a reliable means to draft replacement personnel, nor adequate medical and transport capabilities. The standard type of transport-vehicle was the "A.T. Cart, a two-wheeled, springless vehicle drawn by two mules at an "official" rate of two-and-a-half miles an hour.[15]

In August 1914, the Amy in India had approximately 235,000 troops (76,000 British and 159,000 Indian) organized into seven and one-third divisions, five cavalry brigades, and other support type units. Although not intended to fight outside of the subcontinent, the Army in India dispatched multiple expeditions to meet its overseas requirements. Expeditionary Force 'A' delivered more than two divisions to Europe and six brigades to Egypt; Expeditionary Forces 'B' and 'C' consisted of at least two brigades on both offensive and defensive operations in East Africa; and Expeditionary Force ‘D’ initially consisted of one division in Iraq, although the force there was later expanded and re-designated the II (Tigris) Corps. The remaining units in India maintained internal security were prepared to go to Iran or Afghanistan if required.

The British were so concerned about the effect of sending soldiers into a Muslim country that they actually sent, on October 16th, the soldiers of Force 'D' from Bombay with a large convoy, which was destined for Egypt. Three days out from port, sealed orders were opened and were found to direct Force 'D' to proceed to Bahrein, and there to await further instructions. Bahrein, an island in the Persian Gulf, some 300 miles from the mouth of the Shatt-al-Arab, was reached without incident two weeks later.

Although the British forces that fought in Iraq generally had capable leadership on the tactical level, their strategic leadership in India and London was initially inept. At the outbreak of the war in August 1914, Winston Churchill, First Lord of the Admiralty, and Lord Kitchener, Minister of War, managed day-to-day operations in consultation with Prime Minister Asquith (1908-1916) and the rest of his Cabinet. Unfortunately, this arrangement during the first critical months of the war “provided no security for quick military decisions, while it offered every inducement to political debate and delay.”

In October, to better maintain central control and prepare plans for future contingencies, Asquith created a War Council that consisted of the Prime Minister, the Secretaries of War,

India, and Foreign Affairs, the Chancellor of the Exchequer, and the First Lord of the Admiralty. Although this Council directed the overall war effort against the Central Powers for the British, the Council did not have day-to-day oversight of the Iraq operation. Asquith changed the name of the Council to the Dardanelles Committee in 1915 and expanded its membership to twelve.[16] Regardless of the oversight mechanisms it tried to employ, Asquith's government did not effectively manage the British war effort in 1914-1915.

In accordance with long-established convention, the British government in India directed and controlled all military operations in that country. Consequently, because of the East India Company's historical commercial activities in the Persian Gulf area, the Viceroy oversaw British interests in Basra prior to the war. Asquith managed the war in Iraq by delegating the responsibility of all operations to Lord Robert Crewe, Secretary of State for India (India Office) in London; Sir Edmund Barrow, the Military Secretary of the India Office; and Lord Charles Hardinge, Viceroy in Dehli. Unfortunately, Crewe and Barrow were not properly staffed to run military operations and they did not receive the necessary information from local commanders in Iraq to make the most informed decisions. Furthermore, there was no clearly established division of responsibility between the India Office and the Viceroy. Both offices either micromanaged details of the operation that should have been decided by the local commander or they neglected to handle policy decisions that should have been formulated at their levels.

Furthermore, General Beauchamp-Duff, Commander-in-

Chief of the Army in India, only answered to the Viceroy in 1914-1915, although the War Office and the General Staff of the Army in India regularly exchanged information on intelligence and technical matters. Kitchener and Beauchamp-Duff communicated directly early in the war, but correspondence was completely cut off after the first few months on "constitutional grounds."[17] After 1914, all direct correspondence had to be coordinated through the Viceroy and the India Office first. This arrangement inevitably led to the omission or delay of communication between Kitchener and Beauchamp-Duff. Similarly, the naval forces required to support amphibious and other land operations in Iraq took orders from the Admiralty in London and its subordinate commands in the East Indies and the Persian Gulf, not the Viceroy.

This command structure adequately served the Viceroy during the Army of India's limited campaigns in Abyssinia (Ethiopia), Afghanistan, Burma, Sudan, and the subcontinent during the nineteenth century.[18] However, it did not function well in the complex, multi-front war that Britain fought in 1914-1918. Ultimately, this non-unified command arrangement greatly complicated the strategy, objectives, and management of British military forces in Iraq. As Lord William Robertson would later comment, "Hence, India never knew from day to day what demands the Home Government might make upon her; the War Office never knew what help India could render or might need; and sometimes it was impossible for anyone to say whether a given question was the business of the War Office or the India Office, or the War Council or the Viceroy."[19]

With this dysfunctional command structure in place, the India Office warned the Viceroy in late September 1914 that he should prepare to send troops to the Basra vilayet in Iraq if the Ottoman Empire joined the Central Powers. No prepared operation plan existed, because of the potential pre-World War I political fallout at home and abroad if it were discovered that Britain had contingencies for operations in the Persian Gulf. The British people would not have tolerated its government formulating plans for a costly overseas expedition in the face of lean economic times at home. Similarly, the Ottoman Empire would have understandably viewed negatively any potential plans to seize its colonial possessions. The British were especially sensitive not to provoke the Ottoman Empire prior to World War I because of their desire to see the Turks remain neutral in any future conflict in Europe. Ironically, shortly prior to World War I, students at the Army in India's staff college in Quetta considered operations against the Ottoman Empire in Iraq as a staff problem. However, the head staff at the college later dismissed possible operations in Iraq due to "the distances and difficulties of communications involved, with the lack of attainable decisive objectives and the forces that would be available."[20]

# CHAPTER 6

# THE BATTLE FOR IRAQ BEGINS

*According to advice offered to British officers with regard to equipping themselves for service in Mesopotamia: "To spend a year in this delectable land you will require three outfits of clothing: one suitable for an English winter; one suitable for an English summer; and an outfit suitable for Hades!"*

The Lower Mesopotamia that the British military found is a flat plain of alluvial clay, unrelieved by hills or single eminence of any importance. Baghdad, five hundred miles from the Persian Gulf, is little more than a hundred feet above sea level and between the capital and the sea lies a vast area of featureless desert, of which the monotony is broken only by the great rivers and the marshes into which they "spill" when they are flooded by the melting snows at far-off mountain sources. Except for the palm groves, which straggle here and there along the banks of the rivers, this inhospitable environment is treeless, stoneless, and away from the rivers, waterless. When dry, the surface of the land is passable by all arms, excepting where deep irrigation channels hinder the passage of wheels, but a few hours of rain turn it into a quagmire of greasy mud through which only small parties of infantry can flounder with difficulty. In the flood season, huge areas of desert are converted into stretches of open water or into impassable morasses. South of the Kut-Kufa line flooded rivers are apt to rise above the level of the surrounding country, so that, to prevent wholesale inundation, great earthworks, or "bunds" (which are very liable to damage) are built at the sides of their courses to hold in their swollen waters.

Between May and October the heat is intense, rising to as much as 134 degrees farenheit in the shade. Away from the sea the heat is dry, but south of Amara, the climate is damp, sticky and unhealthy. Between November and April, the weather is cool, and in the months December to March it can be decidedly cold. The change from six months of intense heat to the days of the winter, when a biting wind drives a cold rain across the desert, is very great and it was felt with particular severity by Indian troops. November to the middle of December are probably the best months of the year, because, unlike the remainder of the cool season, they are not liable to violent storms of wind and cold rain. After even a few hours of rain, the whole country becomes a sea of glutinous mud which makes movement of troops almost impossible. In extreme heat, airplanes cannot fly between the hours of about 9am. and 5pm because of the difficulty of climbing through the layers of rained air which is super-heated by radiation from the ground, and in wet weather, pilots cannot always rely on taking off from the mud.

Of all the characteristic features of Mesopotamia, perhaps "mirage" was the most remarkable. In the open desert, troops would appear to advance, to recede, to become invisible; a small bush would turn into a platoon of infantry; a few sheep would become a squadron of cavalry; at a distance of a thousand yards, quite large bodies of troops might be invisible, while at three or four hundred yards it was not always possible to distinguish objects, or even to be sure if an object existed. Whatever its form, mirage is a most disconcerting accompaniment to military operations, because it interferes with reconnaissance, with observation of fire and with visual signaling.

From a health standpoint, Iraq has little to recommend it. Apart from the very trying climatic conditions, health is threatened by disease: plague, smallpox, malaria, sandfly fever, dysentery, and Baghdad boils (this last, a most dispiriting and un-decorative affliction), cholera, typhus, scurvy, and heat-stroke. Sickness is spread by insects, mosquitoes, sandflies, and (until the hot weather kills them) incredible numbers of, flies.

This inhospitable region first entered the strategic realm on August 25, 1914 with a requirement for the India Office to prepare a ground force to guard the scattered refineries of the Anglo-Persian Oil Company from Abadan Island and gunboats to secure the Shatt-al-Arab estuary. This mission in modern parlance was a force deterrent option (FDO). The 16th Indian Brigade Group under Brig. Gen. W. S. Delamain reached Bahrain on October 23, 1914.

On October 29th, the Ottoman Empire attacked Russia in the Black Sea and on November 5th, Great Britain declared war on Turkey. On the 31st, the British Admiralty ordered the Chief of Naval Forces in the Persian Gulf to do the following: commence hostilities against the Turks; proceed up the Shatt-al-Arab to protect oil facilities in Abadan; and to land the expeditionary troops at Fao, just south of Basra. On the next day, General Delamain also received orders from the Viceroy to land his forces in Fao, in concert with naval authorities and to await reinforcements. Although the Admiralty and the India Office consulted on events in Iraq, the taskings for the Army and Navy were issued in separate orders and the details of coordinating the joint operation were ultimately left to British authorities in theater. Without a doubt, this was an operational design that resulted in the lack of effective coordination and efficient management of resources.

When Britain declared war on the Ottoman Empire, the Army in India's Expeditionary Force 'D' consisted of 4,731 officers and men. The Force arrived off the bar of the Shatt-al-Arab on November 3rd and on the 6th a small contingent of Royal Marines and three companies of Indian troops landed on the Fao peninsula and captured the fort where it destroyed the ramparts and threw its guns into the river. The Force then proceeded up river to Sanniyah, opposite the oil works at Abadan, where on November 8th it set up a camp and beating off a Turkish counter-attack with assistance of the mountain batteries, dug in to await reinforcements. By November 10th, Expeditionary Force 'D' had landed its entire force without any significant resistance, and on November 13th, General Sir Arthur Barrett took command of the entire force. On November 17th, the 16th and 18th Brigades attacked Ottoman forces near Sahil, located south of Basra. Heavy rain had turned the ground to a quagmire, but the Turks were driven out with heavy losses, suffering over 1,500 casualties. The remaining Turks fled and Barrett broke off the pursuit since he lacked airplanes and cavalry, and tended to his own casualties, approximately 489 killed and wounded, strewn out on the desert battlefield.[21]

If the seizure of oil facilities at Abadan seemed logical to the British, it came as a complete surprise to the Turks. Because of Britain's limited military assets and the threat posed by the Germans in continental Europe, the Turks did not expect a British assault in Iraq. As an undated Ottoman Army document captured during the war aptly put, "How could England, with its little Army, add aggressive action against the Turks to her contest with the German millions?"[22]

In fact, the Turks were so confident that the British would never attack, they reduced the number of their troops in Iraq, sending a significant number of their forces to Syria and Erzerum, Turkey. They believed that the use of locally drafted forces and collaborative tribes would be sufficient to help the remaining regular forces defend Iraq from any internal or external threats.

By late October, just before war was declared between Britain and the Ottoman Empire, the Turks only had 17,000 rifles (soldiers), 380 sabres (cavalry), forty-four artillery pieces, and three machine guns in Iraq, and these forces were considered poor quality by even Ottoman standards. "The [Ottoman] troops [in Iraq] are described as being below establishment, ill-trained, ill-disciplined, and badly equipped, with no proper organization for supply and maintenance. Desertions were many and at one time, in Baghdad, they amounted to 1,200 in one day."[23]

Preparations were then made to deal with the next Turkish position at Baljaniya, but the victory at Sahil clearly had a negative effect on Turkish morale for on November 20th news arrived that the Turks had abandoned Baljaniya and Basra, and were retiring on Al-Amara. An advance force embarked on river craft and arrived at Basra on November 21st and the main force followed overland, enduring a very wearying march, and arrived late on November 22nd. The Division made a ceremonial entry into Basra on November 23rd, raising the Union Flag over the principal buildings, accompanied by a salute from the guns of the warships. The population received the British with mixed feelings. "Although openly they expressed pleasure at our arrival, their misgivings lest the Turks should ultimately return imbued their welcome with caution."

When the British entered Basra the town was being looted and all the peaceful citizens were either in hiding or had placed themselves on the defensive. A proclamation was instantly posted calling upon the people to preserve order and to observe certain rules. It decreed that all looting must stop and said that robbery under arms, and certain other crimes, would be punished by established and well-known military methods.

But it happens that robbery under arms has been one of the principal Arab industries for ages, so it was not easy to make a decree against it effective. As the British found, there was hardly an Arab who did not possess a gun, and many of them had well-stocked arsenals, as the British discovered when they began a systematic search for arms. It is said that the average Arab's highest ambition in life is to become the owner of a good rifle and one hundred rounds of ammunition, for with a good rifle' and one hundred rounds of ammunition he can go raiding, have a wonderful time, and make that kind of living for an indefinite period. Or he can join the "army" of some desert chieftain, be taken care of, and have all the wild excitement his heart desires.

There was one case of robbery under arms after another, and since the troops were so busy elsewhere, adequate patrol could not be provided, making conditions intolerable. So when a robber was caught red-handed one night in the act of holding up two Arab dancing-girls who were on their way home with their earnings from a party at which they had performed, the general officer commanding decided that instead of sending him for a long period to a jail that was already overcrowded, he would have him publicly flogged in the open square. He would make an example of him and put the fear of the wrath of the British in the hearts of his brethren.

The population was advised that the terrible exhibition was to take place and the locals gathered at the appointed hour in full force. When everything was in readiness, the culprit was led forth and strapped into place.

The British expected everybody to be horrified. However, the girls who had been the victims of the robber, and on whose account he was to undergo this most ignominious of all punishments, had brought a number of friends to see the show and had disposed themselves comfortably in a long window which commanded a perfect view. They were all dressed up and perched on a bench, giggling and having the time of their young lives.

The British major who had charge of the proceedings said that he felt all the time as though he were standing on a volcano of mirth that was likely to explode at any moment.

He gave the command for the floggers to proceed, but just

at that moment, the bench on which the girls were squatting gave way and they all fell backward, some of them with their feet waving in the air, and the crash was the signal for a roar of laughter from all sides. The wretched creature strapped to the flogging-board and with a stripe or two already laid across his back, raised his head and joined in with the utmost heartiness, while the floggers and the British soldiers, in their amusing efforts to keep their faces straight, added to the general fiasco.

After that they decreed that hanging should be the punishment for robbery under arms, and the next scene in the public square was not so merry. After two hangings in full view of the whole population. robbery and thieving in the vicinity of Basra suddenly ceased. It was as though the Arabs said to the Englishman: "Oh, well if you are as serious as all that about it!"

The Turkish army was divided into three sections with one of these under Subhi Bey, a former Wali (military governor) of the Basra district, fortified in a strong position at Qurna, about forty-six miles to the north, where a branch of the Euphrates flows into the Tigris. Here Subhi Bey was in easy communication with Baghdad and could be rapidly reinforced.

However, the main Turkish force, under Suleiman Askeri, was concentrating on the Euphrates for a massed descent via the old stronghold of Shaiba, which lies about twelve miles northwest of Basra and was held at that time by a mere handful of British troops.

The third section, amounting to eight battalions and some ten thousand well-armed Arabs, was organized on the Karun River in Persia, threatening the Anglo-Persian oil-fields and seriously undermining the power of the loyal Sheikh of Muhammerah by disaffecting thousands of his tribesmen either through bribery or by religious misrepresentation.

So, to establish security for their position, the British were compelled to resume offensive operations, and at once, the object being to drive the enemy back on all sides to points as far removed as possible from the borders and coasts along which lay Britain's greatest danger. After the capture of Basra, Sir Percy Cox, the political officer attached to the British forces, sent a private telegram to the Viceroy saying "after earnest consideration of the arguments for and against I find it difficult to see how we can well avoid taking over Baghdad."

From a military point of view, to contemplate any significant advance with a force of one division, considering the operational circumstances in which the Expedition was placed was almost impossible. The only course dictated by sound strategy was the course which General Barrett recommended, and that was, to consolidate his position at Basra. In India, the General Staff stated that an advance to Baghdad, even if it were feasible, would entail a diversion of military resources to an objective of secondary importance, and that "however desirable politically, military considerations indicate that even success would result in our general strategic position being weakened rather than strengthened..."

However, Colonel Cox's opinion had considerable effect in India, where in political circles any chance to increase British prestige in Mohammedan eyes, and any opportunity to check the flow of anti-British propaganda into Persia, Afghanistan, and the

North West Frontier, were hailed with enthusiasm. At the India Office, too, political opinion strongly favored Colonel Cox's proposal with the Political Secretary going so far as to say that he regarded the step as being so desirable as to be practically essential." In fact, no sooner was the idea of an advance to Baghdad mentioned than it became an obsession in political circles.

At the India Office, the Military Secretary, although he admitted that a policy of passivity was inappropriate because it would fail to impress the Arab and Indian public, gave as his considered opinion that any thought of an immediate advance to Baghdad was premature. He suggested however, that to advance to Qurna was within the capabilities of General Barrett's force and that the step would be one which would consolidate the position at Basra, strengthen hold on the oilfields area, and create in the mind of the enemy the idea that the British were contemplating a future advance upon Baghdad.

Qurna is at the junction of the old course of the Euphrates and the Tigris, and is the reputed site of the Garden of Eden. It dominates the navigable waters, telegraph lines and the rich cultivated lands of the Shatt-al-Arab, and it overlooks Persian Arabistan and their oilfelds.

After a reconnaissance by the Navy, General Barratt gave the task of capturing Qurna to 18th Brigade. On December 4th, the battalions landed on the east bank below Qurna and advanced towards the Tigris through the village of Muzereh and the surrounding date plantations. Although the troops captured the village and reached the bank of the River, they came under effective fire and could not cross, so withdrew at nightfall to their landing point and sent for the rest of the Brigade. The attack was repeated on December 7th with the whole of brigade, but with the same result, except that they only withdrew as far as the village. That night they sent for a bridging detachment. On December 8th, while the sloops bombarded the enemy in Qurna, troops moved north of the town to select a bridging site. Once a suitable site was found, Sergeant Halvidar Ghulam swam the river with a line and a flying bridge (a form of ferry using the current to drag the boats across) was quickly established, by which the rest of the battalion crossed and formed up ready to advance.

Further up the river, troops were able to cross in an unattended makhaila (river boat) and the two battalions joined up to advance on the town. Coming up against the main defenses, the commanding officers decided it was too late to start an action that would involve a running fight in the plantations and streets at night, so preparations were made to attack next day. However, cut off from his line of retreat and bombarded by the ships, the Turkish commander, General Subhi Bey, sent out for terms and surrendered next morning with 42 officers and 1,000 men, having already suffered over 1,000 casualties.

General Barratt's force had now achieved its immediate objectives and secured the oilfields and refinery.

For the rest of the winter the troops fortified their positions at Qurna and Shaiba, protecting Basra from attack from the south and west, and securing the west bank of the Shatt-al-Arab to the sea. It was a fairly unpleasant and relatively uneventful winter (1914 – 1915) with the troops standing only a few feet above the surrounding floods and wallowing in mud.

Meanwhile the telegraph wires between London, Delhi and Basra were humming as the government decided what to do next. Clearly the Turks would not tolerate the loss of Basra for long and would mount a counter-attack as soon as they were able.

In an attempt to spread insurrection and chaos throughout Muslim areas held by the British, French, and Russian territory, Sultan Mehmed V declared "holy war" in Constantinople on November 11th, promoting the killing of all Christians who did not have German nationality.[24] This fatwa (religious decree) was one element of Germany's "Drang Nach Osten" or "Push to the East" where Berlin hoped it could eclipse Britain's military and economic dominance.

Berlin and Constantinople subsequently dispatched agents to both Persia and Afghanistan to try to convince national leaders to shed their neutrality and join the Central Powers. While one tribe, the Bawi, rose and cut the pipe-line which connected the oilfields with the refineries, ultimately, the efforts to spread religious rebellion failed. "Mehmed V's holy war was a flop."[25] Although scattered Muslim units in the British Army did rebel during World War I, this was more resulting from their deployment outside of India rather than a general rebellion against British rule. Britain's Muslim subjects may not have appreciated London's rule, but they did not seek to replace it with Ottoman rule either.

There was also a presumption by the British that if the

Arabs were to be won over, they then needed to extend their hold over Lower Mesopotamia and give the impression they were here to stay.

In February, 1915 information was received that the Turks had left Al-Amara heading for the oilfields at Ahwaz, and that the pipeline had been cut. To counter this move, and to ensure that the Arabs did not turn against the British, General Barratt sent Brigadier General Robinson and a force north of Ahwaz. On March 3rd, he was ambushed and forced into a fighting withdrawal. Lt Staples reported the battle in a letter to his parents:

> Well at 2am on 3rd March we were marched out, a force of less than 1,000 men all told to make 'reconnaissance in force'. We had two field guns and two mountain guns. About 6am we got to a place about three miles from the Arab camps and it got light, so we wished them good morning by plumping shells into the camps. We watched the Arabs with our glasses come buzzing out like a disturbed wasps nest and thought they were going to run away. We all felt sorry for them when we saw the shells bursting on them – however they didn't run away but produced green, red and white banners. Then they proceeded to advance upon us from three sides simultaneously and very rapidly and rifle fire soon started. We were all ordered to retire, which we proceeded to do … I never expected to get back to camp as we were being pelted with bullets from never less

> than three sides all the time and were cruelly outnumbered – two things to my mind saved us – one was the surprising inaccuracy of the Arabs' fire … the second was that they never had the pluck to push us and cut us all down, which I am sure they could have done … I never saw anything so absolutely steady as those few men of the Dorsets. It really was a joy to see them. The RFA too were grand.[26]

Meanwhile rumors had started that the Turks were planning a counter offensive on Basra so a reconnaissance was made up the Tigris to Ruta but it was discovered that the river was blocked and defenses firmly held south of the town. During the first week of April local tribes reported that a Turk-Arab concentration, which was estimated to be some twelve thousand Regular Turkish troops and ten thousand Arab Irregulars, was taking place around Nasiriyeh. At the same time the outpost at Ahwaz was attacked. The Turks were under the command of Colonel Suleiman Askari, an energetic commander who had made his name in Bulgaria, but was still recovering from wounds received at Qurna.

With great difficulty another Indian Division, the 12th, consisting of the 12th, 33rd, and 30th Infantry Brigades (the last from Egypt) but without its full complement of Divisional Artillery, Engineers and Signalers was mobilized and sent to Mesopotamia.

# CHAPTER 7

# THE MIRACLE OF SHAIBA

Supplying the British force was difficult because the whole area between Basra and Shaiba was flooded waist deep, with a deep channel that made wading impossible. To supply the troops, a combination of mules and bellums (shallow draught native boats) traveling on different routes had to be used. Adding to the difficulties, the port facilities in Basra could not support extended operations. With "practically no quays or wharfage, vessels were unloaded in midstream by primitive methods into native sailing craft. There were no warehouses available for the storage of goods, and accommodation for troops was also lacking."[27] Basra also lacked the basic infrastructure (e.g., roads, hospitals, and sanitation services, etc.) to adequately support the movement of large numbers of men and material moving north.

The Turkish operations to recapture Basra opened on March 31, 1915 with simultaneous bombardments of Shaiba and Qurna. At Qurna, the bombardment of the 6th British (Poona) Division progressed for three days while periodic attempts at piercing the town's defenses were unsuccessful. Eventually a counter-attack by the 2nd Dorsets and 24th Punjabis routed the Turks with heavy losses.

Suleiman Askari advanced south towards Basra moving west of the flooded area. On April 10th, British cavalry patrols made contact with the enemy but withdrew in the face of superior numbers, while the Turks made for Barjisiyeh Wood, four miles to the west of Shaiba.

At 6:15am on April 11th, the British set off to Shaiba. Most of the march was across flooded desert, with the men wading through water varying in depth from six inches to five feet. By the time they arrived they were close to collapse, hungry and thirsty, soaked with sweat and water, and then as the freezing cold of night fell. The British force consisted of three regiments of cavalry, eight infantry battalions and four batteries of artillery, including one of horse and one of mountain guns.

The British position at Shaiba was laid out in a large semi-circle facing west with its base resting on the edge of the floods. The 3-mile long defenses were an irregular line of trenches with the Shaiba Fort at its center, the Kiln Post, a 60 foot-high brick kiln, to the north, and the South Salient to the south. To the north were some houses and beyond that a low ridge, the North Mound. The whole area was flat, open and treeless.

The attack opened at dawn on April 12th and for the next three days the two armies attacked and counter-attacked to gain advantage.

General Melliss and his Brigade moved into position at Shaiba, under the watchful eyes of the local population that assembled to welcome back the Turks. As the senior General, he was to take command, but as the fighting was still going on, he chose to wait till daylight. He writes the following in a letter:

> Nixon [who had arrived from India on April 8th to take over command from General Barrett] decided to send me out with one battalion in canoes. A large

> number were collected and by 4pm I started, you should have seen my fleet! The men poling and of course awkwardly being new to it. It was a very scattered fleet, as we drew near Shaiba camp the enemy tried to shell us but it was getting dark and they could not get the range. About 8pm I arrived and some of my divisional staff in the leading canoes. It was quite dark incessant firing going on all around for the enemy was attacking. We were afraid of being shot by our own side or by the Turk, however we got inside the defences alright, my canoe man being shot in the arm. Bullets were flying all over the camp, maxims going, star shell rising in the air and falling in blue green lights to show up the enemy. It was picturesque but unpleasant.[28]

On April 13th Turkish troops attempted to outflank the British across the floods that separated Shaiba from Basra, and their cavalry prepared for a frontal assault. At 7am, the British Cavalry Brigade attacked the North Mound, but after stiff fighting in which Major Wheeler was killed trying to capture an Arab standard, for which he was awarded the VC, the Brigade withdrew. General Melliss describes the battle:

> Chitty took me to what must have been an old Babylonish tower which stood near his part of the defences. That tower proved my good friend and was the cause of my good fortune. The whole situation lay before me, there were thousands of Turks and Arab

> riflemen on all three sides of us at a distance of a mile and nearer in some places, behind trenches in houses and holding sandy ridges they simply swarmed, and there was the cavalry brigade just moving out! It was too late I could not stop them. One cavalry regiment made a gallant charge against a body of the enemy on a sand hill with their standards stuck on the crest. They drove some of the Arabs before them and got into them with the lance but the fire was too hot on all sides and they had to fall back leaving Major Wheeler and an Indian officer dead on the mound where the standards were, they had ridden most gallantly at it to seize the standards. The rest of the cavalry brigade were fired into from the flank and had to retire too. I then sent for General Delamain and ordered him out with three battalions … to attack the mound and the house etc. in its vicinity and I got up my old friend Colonel Cleeve on to the mound where we overlooked everything and told him to support the infantry with all the guns. From there we switched them on to whatever point we wished. It was as we just pounded them with shells and under cover of it the infantry advanced and captured the enemy's position and houses with little loss. The houses were blown up and over 90 dead were found on one mound called the north mound.[30]

Turkish attacks on the South Salient during the morning were repulsed with little difficulty. At noon General Melliss ordered his troops to sweep round to the west and south of Shaiba to clear the front, and capture the enemy guns that had been abandoned. Major-General C.L Fry issued the order, "Push forward at all costs and take enemy trenches." Colonel Peebles drew his sword (it was one of the last occasions on which officers carried swords in action) and launched his men into the attack with the shout, "Come on the 2nd!"

The 2nd Battation, Norfolk Regiment advanced over 500 yards of featureless desert with machine gun and rifle bullets zipping about their ears. They charged, heedless of fire and casualties, yelling to keep their hearts from pumping out of their mouths. The Turks, shaken by the wildness of the charge, fled from them, and the mile long ridge which was the Shaiba position became the property of the Norfolks. It was a clear-cut victory, but a costly one to the Battalion in dead and wounded.

Lt H C West of S Battery describes the battle:

> Our infantry had to attack down an absolutely open glacis leading to the wood against an entrenched enemy whom they could not see, the mirage making things much worse. They behaved simply splendidly, natives as well as British, and walked solemnly on down this slope under a most murderous fire. They lost pretty heavily, but went on perfectly steadily. The field artillery were firing over their heads in one place, where they were only fifty yards from the enemy. The battery commanders were in an awful funk about hitting our own people. However, the infantry sent back to say they

> would rather have their fire and risk a few of our own shells coming into them. The Turkish rearguard hung on most stubbornly. With the accurate artillery fire on them, they simply could not get up to go; anyhow, they lay there and fired away till eventually our infantry got right into them. In their last trench practically every man was killed. Their rearguard put up a most stubborn fight and enabled the rest to get away, as by the time our infantry had practically wiped it out they were too exhausted to follow up the main body.[31]

By the end of the day the troops were exhausted and short of ammunition. General Melliss declined to attack the enemy on the South Mound and withdrew the brigade back to the main encampment where the force spent a quiet night. On April 14th the Turks had withdrawn to Barjisiyeh Wood and General Melliss was able to go on to the offensive. His anxiety and relief is clear from his letter to his wife:

> The fight lasted from 10.30 to 5 p.m. I never want to go through the anxiety of some of that time, reports came into me of heavy losses on all sides and doubt if further advance was possible. I had thrown in my last man into the fight – still it hung very doubtful, I could see through the mirage with difficulty movements of masses beyond the woods, probably the Kurds and Arabs but whether retreating or coming on it was impossible to say. At last came a time when word came that our gun ammunition was running out! There was

> nothing for it but to prepare plans for retiring (can you imagine my feelings!) one of the two regiments left to guard the camp was ordered out and all transport carts also to collect wounded and I sent word to the brigadiers to come to me to receive [orders] about falling back. When to my joy a report came to me that the Dorsets and others had carried the enemy's first line of trenches some 900 [yards] in front of the wood and that they were on the run. Can you imagine how thankful I felt.[32]

This sudden reversal of fortune became known as the Miracle of Shaiba. By 5pm the Turks had abandoned the position and were fleeing to the north making a fine target for the artillery. Reluctant to remain away from his base after dark, surrounded by marauding Arabs, General Melliss ordered the force to retire to Shaiba. They need not have feared however, for the Arabs, sensing they had backed the wrong side, had turned on their erstwhile allies and harried their retreat mercilessly. The whole force was back in camp by 8:30pm, having suffered 1,000 casualties, of which 161 were killed. The mule drivers were especially commended for their bravery in re-supplying the infantry under fire. Suleiman Askari, who had conducted the battle from his sickbed in the Wood, summoned his officers and, cursing their incompetence and the treachery of the Arabs, shot himself rather than see the ruin of his project. The Turks withdrew in confusion to Khamisiyah then Nasiriyah.

The British were not at first aware of the full extent of their victory at Shaiba, but the battle had: cleared the western approaches to Basra of a dangerous menace; restored the initiative to the British; and, bought time to decide on the next course of action.

General Nixon had a number of choices: to follow up his success with an advance on Nasiriyah, but he had insufficient river craft, no information, and there was no immediate threat; to advance on Al Amara for which there were again insufficient river craft, but it would secure the oilfields; or to advance on Ahwaz to secure the oilfield and his eastern flank, and to reassure the Sheik of Mohammerah, although the heat and desert would make for a difficult campaign.

This last was the most immediate threat, so General Nixon ordered General Gorringe to advance on Ahwaz and drive the Turks out of Arabistan, where they had massed 5,000 troops and an equal number of Arab auxiliaries. Meanwhile, General Nixon turned his attention to the capture of Al Amara and closing the Turks' route into Arabistan.

# CHAPTER 8

# BEYOND SHAIBA

The formation of the II Indian Army Corps, and the appointment of General Nixon to command it, mark a distinct turning-point in the history of the campaign. General Nixon, a cavalry soldier, a polo-player, and a pig-sticker, had a well-earned reputation for dash, being energetic, and inclined to the Napoleonic in his decisions. He was more a natural leader than a highly trained commander, consequently he was, perhaps, somewhat prone to regard war as an affair in which the "practical man" who was not afraid of accepting personal responsibility, could achieve his end by ordinary "common-sense" untrained methods. He saw everything from the fighting point of view, leaving the operational aspects to take care of themselves.

General Nixon, not unnaturally, read into the instructions of the Commander-in-Chief an intended change of policy, nor was his Staff, which was to some extent improvised from inexperienced and untrained personnel, likely to be able to advise restraint to a commander whose chief characteristic was a keen desire to push on at all costs. Consequently, when charged with the spirit of the offensive after his victory at Shaiba, fired by the thought of Baghdad as an objective, he at once conceived a vigorous plan of action, with which his political adviser, always anxious to increase British prestige in the eyes of the Arabs, was in full sympathy.

By contrast, the opinion of the Secretary of State for

India was that British policy in Mesopotamia should continue to be limited to its original objectives, and that strategic action should be confined to the measures necessary to defend the Basra vilayet and securing the oilfields, pipe-line and refineries. To him, the situation as it then existed seemed well in hand, and, as no reinforcements were available for the Expedition, he felt that "we must play a safe game in Mesopotamia…" and not seek to extend the existing sphere of operations excepting, perhaps, by a purely local offensive on the Karun or up the Tigris towards Amara if by doing so we should be materially contributing to the security of the oil-supply.

Under these guidelines, General Nixon considered three alternative courses of action. He could follow up the remnants of the Turkish Army which, broken at Barjisiyeh, had retired to Nasiriyeh, an important tribal centre; he could attack the enemy on the Tigris and occupy Amara, thus cutting Turkish communications with Northern Arabistan and the oilfields area, and simultaneously giving the impression that he meant to advance on Baghdad; or he could operate in Arabistan to clear the oilfields area and to protect his own right flank against a turning movement. Of the three courses, General Nixon considered the one best calculated to stabilize the situation in the oilfields area was to advance to Amara, a center from which trade routes radiated into Arabistan, and from which the control of the turbulent Beni Lam tribesmen might be successfully exercised.

General Nixon instructed Major General Charles Townshend, newly arrived on April 23rd, to drive the Turks out of their positions north of Qurna and advance on Al Amara. These were aggressive orders to give considering that the hot weather was upon him; that his force was short of transport, tents, medical equipment and supplies; that the operation was in broken desert without adequate communications, and that no increase in his forces were possible.

Upon arriving at Qurna, Townshend found the garrison, the 6th Indian Division, wallowing in mud and surrounded by floods, which, early in the month, were actually two feet above the level of the camp. Between the British at Qurna and the "island" positions which the Turks were occupying on a general line of slightly higher ground, stretched a vast area which was flooded to an average depth of about three feet, although where irrigation canals occurred, the water was as much as twenty feet deep.

General Townshend recognized that this would be an amphibious operation, so he had his infantry trained to maneuver the bellums, with each battalion having about sixty of these craft and about two hundred men specially practiced in propelling them. Covering fire for the infantry "bellum-brigade" was to be provided by the naval flotilla of river gun-boats and by batteries of field artillery carried on rafts, while special rafts not unlike Noah's Arks were constructed to carry field ambulances. Towards the end of May, all General Townshend's preparations were complete, and on the 31st, his force moved out across seven thousand yards of flooded open desert, without cover from view or fire, to attack the Turkish positions.

The Turks were firmly established on a line from Abu

Aran through Muzaibila to Ruta, with advanced positions on Norfolk Hill, One Tree Hill, One Tower Hill and the Sandhills. The artillery bombardment opened at 5am and at 6am the flotilla set out towards the enemy positions. By 6:30am the British had captured One Tree Hill, by 7:30am Norfolk Hill, and One Tower Hill by 9:30am. By 11:30am the Turkish garrison on Gun Hill surrendered to the approaching army.

The troops advanced cautiously across the floods when an airplane scouting ahead dropped a message reporting that Abu Aran, Muzaibilia and Ruta had all been abandoned by the enemy and the Turks were fleeing northwards. At 3pm the flotilla set off in pursuit of the fleeing Turks, though only a rough chart of the river was available. They soon caught up with the Turkish river craft, which cast off the barrages full of troops, leaving them floundering in the water and pleading to be taken prisoner rather than be left to the mercy of the Arabs. At 8pm, when it was too dark to navigate safely, the flotilla anchored for the night, having captured over 200 Turks and three guns.

By June 3rd, General Townshend had now way outpaced his division and was becoming increasingly isolated in the middle of enemy territory with only a small force. While he insisted on pausing twelve miles short of Al Amara, he was encouraged by Captain Nunn to advance cautiously to within three miles of Al Amara. Once there, they saw a pontoon bridge and a steamer loading troops, so The Shaitan steamed ahead, burst through the bridge, and took the surrender of 1,000 Turks.

The Turks were marched back to Al Amara where they "sat by a coffee shop until time could be found to take them into custody." At 1:30pm Townshend arrived and took the surrender of the Governor and Commandant. The prisoners, which now included the force from Arabistan, were secured on barrages and in the barracks. The 41 members of the British force spent an anxious night lest the Turks realize how few their numbers were. At 6:30am next morning, just as the Turks were becoming aware how small the force holding them captive was, the leading companies of the Norfolks arrived to secure the town and its prisoners, to Townshend's immense relief:

> Three shells burst quite close to me standing by the guns, but I came to no harm, and you may believe me when I say how much I enjoyed the whole thing – my first battle in command of a large force of troops and war vessels … About forty to fifty Turkish officers, including their general, surrendered and gave up their swords and arms to myself and twenty-two men, and I wondered why they did not fall upon me and kill me. I gave them an awful telling off in French for not having men's rations and biscuits in their stores at Amara, because I said: 'Here are all my troops arriving and I am short of food,' and I called them a lot of lazy Turks for not having proper food management. You never saw such a scene as I made – and my language! All acted, for not a soldier could arrive for nearly two days, and I was in a nice hole if they found out! ... In the morning just as they all found out I had no one with me, the first transport with the Norfolk Regiment steamed in. There

was great cheering, and then I laid down and slept.[33]

With Al Amara now secured and Ahwaz held by General Nixon, only the capture Nasiriyah, which had been the headquarters of the old Turkish Civil Administration of the district, at the south end of the Shatt-al-Hai, was required to complete the objective of establishing British control in the Basra vilayet. General Nixon gave the task to General Gorringe, now returned from Arabistan, and at the same time, Nixon was trying to win over the powerful Muntafik tribe that dominated the Lower Euphrates.

The British set out for Nasiriyah on June 26th, with the only practical access by way of the Old Channel of the Euphrates from Qurna across Hammar Lake and up the Akaika Channel. However, passage would be exceedingly difficult because the Akaika Channel was dammed with a pre-war irrigation systems and the water levels were now falling.

On June 27th, the force crossed the Hammar Lake to the entrance to the Akaika Channel and reached the dam where a few shots drove off the defending Turkish gunboat. Next day the dam was blown and the channel widened, which allowed the British to pass through, however, with considerable difficulty against the current.

The Turkish position above the Asani Bend was a strong one, with entrenchments on both banks protected by creeks. A detailed reconnaissance on July 7th established that both a frontal and a flanking attack would be difficult. General Gorringe now had only 1,900 fit troops and needed to finish the campaign quickly as the water levels in the rivers were falling and the flotilla was needed elsewhere. He sent for reinforcements while he carried out probing attacks to discover the extent of the Turkish position, which was held by 6,000 troops with 10 guns. Reinforcements arrived between July 11 - 13 and beat off a Turkish spoiling attack. General Gorringe's plan was to seize the Sandhills and Zukhair, then attack on both banks. The attack on Zukhair was successful, however, the attack by on the Sandhills was beaten off with heavy loss, as Melliss recorded:

> On the 14th my Brigade was detailed to make turning movement through the marshes against the enemy's right in order to seize a sort of island from which we could take the Turkish position in rear by gun and rifle fire, of course the movement had to be carried out with the men in native canoes (called Bellums) which hold about ten men and are poled or paddled through the marshes which vary in depth from 2 to 4 feet and sometimes of water with clay and mud at bottom. I had made my arrangements to carry this out when the GOC (Gorringe) changed the plan and said he would prefer the movement to be carried out by one battalion only and detached the 24th Punjabis for it supported by four guns of the mountain battery. Alas with disastrous results - the 24th by canoeing through the night arrived by dawn some 1000 yards from the island in the marshes and proceeded to advance against it on foot through the mud and water of the marshes, all

> went pretty well (although men were exhausted with the heavy wading) until they got within 200 yards of the island when their attack was blasted by hot fire from trenches held by the Turks, our poor fellows were shot down right and left trying to charge the position.[34]

General Gorringe then sent for further reinforcements, which arrived on July 20th after a trying journey through the falling water levels. Gorringe's second attack, on July 24th, again involved parallel attacks on both banks, supplemented by the navy towing an armored bridge into position on the Madanina Creek. This was successful and by 10am the Turks were streaming back to Sadanwiyah. The British followed in river boats under the cover of heavy gunfire from the flotilla, forcing the Turks out of Sadanwiyah by 4pm. Captain Nunn advanced as far as Nasiriyah, but waited till next day to accept the invitation of the Arabs to occupy the town.

In this narrow belt of comparatively dry ground General Gorringe's troops fought for six weary weeks, creeping forward, yard by yard, from sodden trench to sodden trench, in a shade temperature of 120 degrees, a moist swampy heat, eaten alive with insects. In his dispatch, General Nixon said "seldom, if ever, have troops been called upon to campaign in such trying heat…"

At this time, in Persia, German influence had gained considerably, and anti-British propaganda and violence was everywhere. The Russians landed a force in Persia at Enzeli, on the south shore of the Caspian Sea. In Afghanistan, a Turko-

German Mission had reached Kabul, and the resultant attitude of the Amir was as yet unknown. In Egypt, there were apprehensions over the Turkish preparations for a fresh offensive against the Suez Canal. In India, a more than usually determined tribal disturbance on the part of the Mohmands had alarmed the Viceroy and increased the apprehensions with which the internal situation was regarded. Finally, the failure of the Dardanelles campaign and the lack of success on the part of the Allies on the Western front seemed to give occasion for a loss of British prestige. Consequently, intensely desirous of increasing British prestige by any possible means, the Secretary of State for India, strongly expressed the importance of an advance to Baghdad, which to him appeared to be a panacea for all political evils.

While uncoordinated with any authority in London or Dehli nor consistent with the intentions of the higher chain-of-command for British forces in southern Iraq, General Beauchamp-Duff, (Commander-in-Chief of the Army in India) prior to Nixon's arrival in Iraq, ordered Nixon to not only consolidate British control of the Basra vilayet and British petroleum facilities in southern Iraq, but also to prepare for offensive operations against Baghdad.

In this environment, the General Staff in India was giving favorable consideration to General Nixon's proposal to advance to Kut. Nixon argued that Kut, standing at the junction of the Tigris and its effluent, the Hai, was a possible potential advanced base for a hostile counter-offensive which might come either along the Tigris to Amara, or by way of the Hai, to Nasiriyeh, the lower Euphrates and Basra. He also contended that this threat, must force him to keep his troops dispersed instead of concentrating them on the Tigris, as was his desire.

The Secretary of State for India more nearly realized the dangers of the proposal and sought to instill caution into the policy, but by this time the Viceroy had made up his mind that Kut was essential to British prestige, and stated that in his opinion (and in the opinion of "the man on the spot") the advance was "strategically desirable and will have a quieting effect upon Persia."

On August 23rd, General Townshend, commanding the 6th Indian Division, was given instructions to effect "the destruction and dispersion of the enemy... and the occupation of Kut." From these and other instructions he appears to have understood that he was at liberty to follow the Turks into Baghdad. On September 11th, General Nixon ordered the advance on Kut to begin, despite no hope of reinforcements, a greater dispersal of his troops, the length of his communications lines, and the high level of sickness among the troops.

The battle was described by Captain Robert Palmer, an officer with the 6th Hants, in a letter to his father as follows:

> The Turks had a very strongly entrenched position at Kut, with 15,000 men and 35 guns. We feinted at their right and then outflanked their left by a night march of twelve miles. (Two brigades did this, while one brigade held them in front.) Then followed a days hard fighting as the outflankers had to storm three redoubts successfully before they could properly enfilade the

position. Just as they had done it, the whole Turkish reserve turned up on their right and they had to turn on it and defeat it, which they did. But by that time it was dark, the troops were absolutely exhausted and had finished all their water. Nobody could tell how far the river was, so the only thing to do was to bivouac and wait for daylight. In the night the Turks cleared out and got away. If we could have pressed on and seized their bridge, we should have almost wiped them out: but it was really wonderful we did as much as we did under the circumstances. Our casualties were 1243, but only 85 killed. The Turkish losses are not known… we captured about 1400 and 12 of the guns… we buried over 400, but don't know how many the local Arabs buried. Our pursuit was delayed by the mud-banks on the river, and the enemy was able to get clear and reform in their next position, about ninety miles further north. We are now concentrating against them and it is authoritatively reported that large reinforcements have been sent from India. This means they intend going for Baghdad. It seems to me rash… but I suppose there is great need to assert our prestige with the Moslem world, even at the expense of our popularity… for B. is a fearfully sacred place.

General Townshend nastily embarked a force and set off in pursuit of the enemy. Meanwhile, the Turks had gone straight back to Ctesiphon, eighty miles above Kut, to occupy a strong position which had already been prepared. Next day the 6th Cavalry Brigade, which was with General Townshend, overtook the enemy's rear guard forty miles above Kut, but by this time the supply situation was so chaotic that a general halt had to be called. It was not until October 5th that the Cavalry Brigade and the River Column reached Aziziyeh, twenty-one miles further on. The maintenance of the force had now become almost impossible and the pursuit was abandoned.

With the campaign in Lower Mesopotamia almost over, Gen Nixon was generous in his praise in his dispatches:

> I cannot praise too highly the skill and determination with which General Gorringe conducted the task assigned to him – nor the gallant and devoted manner in which the troops under his command responded to the strenuous calls which were made upon them.
>
> Seldom, if ever, have our troops been called upon to campaign in more trying heat than they have experienced this summer in the marshy plains of Mesopotamia… Nor can I fail to express my deep appreciation of the valuable and whole-hearted cooperation of the Royal Navy… It was in a great measure due to their excellent work that these amphibious operations were brought to so successful conclusion.[35]

To which the King replied:

> The splendid achievements of General Gorringe's column in spite of many hardships and the intense heat fills me with admiration.[36]

The campaign to secure the Basra vilayet was thus brought to a successful conclusion. The Turks had been driven out and the oilfields and refineries had been secured, a serious counter attack had been beaten off, and the locations where threats to the infrastructure could be mounted, had also been secured.

By late September 1915, lead elements were now only 200 miles or 320 kilometers south of Baghdad.

# CHAPTER 9

# ONTO BAGHDAD

By the time of the victory at Kut and the pursuit to Aziziyeh, the II Indian Army Corps had become greatly dispersed and now lay scattered over the theatre of operations. At and above Kut was the striking force, composed of General Townshend's 6th Indian Division, the 6th Cavalry Brigade, a small proportion of artillery and divisional troops, and a portion of an extra infantry brigade for line communication duties. Behind this force, small detachments from the 12th Indian Division were strung out along the Tigris to Basra, where the Inspector General of Communications had his Headquarters, and where there were two battalions of infantry and some technical and administrative units; at Nasiriyeh there was a "mixed brigade" from the 12th Division; in Arabistan there was a regiment of cavalry and two companies of infantry, and at Bushire there was a detachment which had been placed under General Nixon's command. The general result of this distribution was that General Nixon had no strategic reserve with which to back up his striking force, nor did it seem at all likely that, in view of the uncertain attitude of the tribes in Arabistan and on the Euphrates, he would be able to carry out his previous intention to withdraw troops from Ahwaz and Nasiriyeh and concentrate them on the Tigris.

However, General Nixon seemed satisfied with the situation, on October 3rd, after the victory at Kut, telegraphed the Commander-in-Chief in India, "I consider I am strong enough to open road to Baghdad" and "with this intention I propose to concentrate at Aziziyeh..." Two days later, he telegraphed that failure to press his advantage would have a bad effect locally on British prestige, that his enemy was demoralized, and could easily be outmaneuvered and destroyed, and that he himself could see nothing which would justify letting slip such an opportunity because from a military point of view, "Baghdad is a focus of Turkish lines of advance of which it is vital to deprive the enemy, apart from any political effect." At Army Headquarters it was pointed out that "politically, failure to seize what appears to be within our grasp would be interpreted as weakness throughout Asia…"

General Nixon then went on to state that the troops he had with him were sufficient to enable him to inflict decisive defeat upon the Turks and to seize Baghdad, but that in order to hold the city he would require reinforcements which, he suggested, should consist of another division of infantry and a regiment of British cavalry.

With forces in striking distance of Baghdad, the Asquith government convened an interdepartmental advisory commission to decide what to do next. The Joint War Office/Admiralty Board, which had no day-to-day oversight of the land operation, and therefore, no knowledge of the poor logistical situation, recommended that: no capture of Baghdad should be attempted; II Corps should be reinforced by two divisions; and this operation should not divert resources from the Western Front. The board recommended a temporary raid on

Baghdad although it is likely they would have ruled out any offensive if they had known the extent of the poor logistical situation.[37]

Motivated by setbacks in Gallipoli and Serbia, and the lack of meaningful progress on the Western Front, the Dardanelles Committee viewed the capture of Baghdad as a potential "striking victory" in their overall struggle against the Central Powers,[40] and ordered the augmentation of Nixon's troops with two divisions from the Western Front.

However, reports from the "War Office, from Egypt and from elsewhere General Nixon learned that Turkish reinforcements were moving from Caucasus, Mosul ("Upper Mesopotamia), and Syria towards Baghdad. Some of these reports were vague, others were contradictory, and at Force Headquarters, which was permanently beset by rumors and counter-rumors, not much attention was paid to them. The intelligence of the local situation, the enemy's strength and dispositions about Ctesiphon, was far too absorbing in interest.

On November 16th General Nixon received a report from the War Office that Khalil's division was reliably reported to have left Bitlis for Baghdad and that an expedition under the command of General von der Golz was on its way to Mesopotamia. On the 19th, General Townshend received local intelligence of the arrival of Turkish reinforcements on the Tigris.

General Nixon, however, remained skeptical. Similar reports had so often proved unfounded that he had come to regard them all as a cry of "wolf," after all, it seemed to him quite probable that this particular news was spread by the enemy to delay his advance. He estimated that the minimum time required for the transfer of troops from Constantinople to Baghdad was eight weeks; and from Bitlis, five. He was of opinion, therefore, that Turkish reinforcements could not arrive in time to interfere with his plans for the immediate future, and he replied to the War Office telegram that he had already had the information a fortnight earlier from his own agents, and that he did not accept it. Nixon and his staff estimated the strength of the Turkish army to be thirteen thousand rifles and thirty-nine guns, and Townshend estimated it as ten thousand nine hundred rifles and thirty guns.

Thus, Nixon, ignorant of the true number of enemy troops on the battlefield, discounting the significance of the logistical shortfalls, and assuming two divisions redeploying from Europe would augment his troops in a timely manner, directed General Townshend, the new 6th Division commander, to start his march on Baghdad by mid-November 1915.[38] Although Townshend warned Nixon of his tenuous supply lines, and detailed the strongly entrenched enemy position near Ctesiphon, he dutifully complied with the order and continued his advance north.[39]

Unfortunately for II Corps, the Turks had indeed significantly reinforced their forces in Iraq and now they had as many as 60,000 troops stationed in and around Baghdad. General Nurettin Pasha took over the newly created 6th Army, which consisted of: the 51st and 52nd Infantry Divisions, both composed of combat veterans, arrived from Constantinople; and, the 45th Infantry Division, composed of former Gendarmerie and frontier type troops. In fall 1915, the Army in India didn't realize that it was facing a reinforced and more capable Turkish Army than it had had ever encountered before.[41]

Townshend's 6th Division advanced north in early November, augmented by two battalions from the 30th Brigade of the 12th Division. In Ctesiphon, approximately twenty miles southeast of Baghdad, Townshend encountered a Turkish force of more than 20,000 combatants who were protected by two lines of deep trenches on both sides of the Tigris River.[42] Captain Robert Palmer described the battle in a letter as follows:

> Well, we attacked, and carried their first line and half their second before darkness pulled us up. A successful day, though expensive in casualties. We bivouacked in their first line. Daybreak revealed the unpleasant surprise of strong enemy reinforcements, who are said to have diddled our spies by avoiding Baghdad: 5,000 of them. As we had started the affair about 12,000 strong to their 15,000, this was serious. They attacked and were driven off. In the afternoon they attacked again, in close formation: our artillery mowed them, but they came on and on, kept it up all night, with ever fresh reinforcements, bringing them to 30,000 strong all told. By dawn our men were exhausted and the position untenable. A retreat was ordered, that meant ninety miles back to Kut over a baked billiard table. The enemy pressed all the way. Once they surrounded our rear brigade. Two officers broke through their front lines

to recall the front lot. Another evening we pitched a camp and left it empty to delay the enemy. Daily rear guard actions were fought. Five feverish days got us back to Kut, without disorder or great loss of men; but the loss in material was enormous. All possible supplies had been brought close up to the firing line to facilitate our pursuit: mainly in barges, the rest in carts. The wounded filled all the carts, so those supplies had to be abandoned. The Tigris is a cork-screwed maze of mud-banks, no river for the hasty withdrawal of congested barges under fire. You can imagine the scene. Accounts differ as to what we lost. Certainly, two gunboats (destroyed), one monitor (disabled and captured), the telegraph barge and supply barge, besides all supplies, dumped on the bank. Most accounts add one barge of sick and wounded (400), the aeroplane barge, and a varying number of supply barges. In men from first to last we lost nearly 5,000: the Turks about 9,000 a guess of course.

The tale of woe is nearly complete. My A Coy got as far as Kut and was set to feverish entrenching and wiring. Now the whole force there, some 8,000 in all, is cut off there and besieged. They have rations (some say half rations) for six weeks or two months, and ammunition. They are being bombarded, and have been attacked once, but repelled it easily. We aren't worried about them. Meanwhile our reinforcements have turned up in great numbers and expect to be able to relieve Kut by the end of the month.

Medical personnel organized for dealing with a few hundred casualties was endeavoring to cope with three thousand five hundred cases. Hospital ships with accommodation for five hundred had been made ready, but these were soon filled with the casualties which came trickling back over the desert before ever the main battle was joined; consequently, when on the night of the 22nd the battle casualties began to arrive, their thin clothing soaked through, and their bodies almost flayed by the bitter wind which was blowing, no room could be found for them. These men, jolted over the rough desert in the springless, cushionless Army Transport Carts which had been improvised as ambulances, so ineffective that wounded men with broken limbs threw themselves out and crawled across the desert on hands and knees rather than endure the agony of the shaking; or they used dead bodies as cushions between them and the bottom of the carts. Small steamers carried as many as six hundred cases for a voyage to Basra of up to thirteen days because of attacks by Arab Irregulars.

The real severity of the situation was appreciated by neither General Nixon nor the Government of India. When the retreat began, General Nixon was still visualizing carrying out an offensive role. If he was going to resume the offensive, he argued, it was desirable to continue to hold Kut as an advance base, and he also said that British prestige would suffer if Townshend continued to retire.

Nixon's views were upheld by the Viceroy, who still

clung strongly to the conviction that to occupy Baghdad was the best means of countering German intrigue in Persia and Afghanistan, and that success in Mesopotamia was the main factor in keeping these countries and India quiet. While approving General Nixon's attitude, he asked the Secretary of State for yet another division to be added to Force 'D' bringing it up to five in all. No one seems to have realized that it was impossible for the river transport of the force to be "immediately augmented" because suitable craft were not in existence, and that neither the base, the communications nor the transport system could possibly be expanded in time effectively to maintain a sudden influx of reinforcements. The operational factors were governing on the strategic situation, a fact that remained unappreciated.

General Nixon said he hoped to effect relief in two months, for which purpose he was going to concentrate his reinforcements at Amara. General Townshend, who had expected to be relieved after, at most, a month, was considerably taken aback by this, and on December 6th he telegraphed to General Nixon saying that to wait two months for relief was to risk being invested by a very large force he estimated at six divisions and that therefore he proposed to withdraw from Kut to All Gharbi, 40 miles above Amara, and to make his stand there, acting as covering force to the main concentration. He said that at Kut his position was unsound because he was confined in a narrow peninsula which could easily be surrounded by the enemy, that his troops were rested and that he still had time to withdraw and to save most of his ammunition and his heavy guns, or alternatively, to destroy them.

General Nixon, who at the time was in very poor health refused to relinquish his idea for a renewed offensive, and telegraphed to Townshend saying he did not approve of the suggested withdrawal to All Gharbi. His reasons were that he considered the estimate of two months for the relief operations was an outside one, as within the next week he would have a brigade of cavalry and a brigade of infantry concentrated at Ali Gharbi behind Townshend; that to withdraw from Kut would open the line of the Hai to a hostile advance, and would be extremely bad for British prestige and morale; and that, as at present the Turks were making no fresh forward movement, it was not a military necessity.

However, on December 7th, General Townshend replied that he was completely reassured by the prospect of the early arrival of troops at Ali Gharbi and that he would remain at Kut. That evening, he reported that bodies of hostile troops had moved down-stream past Kut on both banks of the river, and that on the left bank up-stream of him there were two divisions of the enemy.

In late December, the Turks launched a heavy attack against Kut, which was beaten off with very great determination. The cost to the Turks was so great that they decided to abandon an active siege and to reduce Kut by blockade alone, and on the 26th with this object in view, they commenced to move more troops down the river on the left bank to interpose them between General Townshend and any force coming up to attempt his relief. Thus, Kut became entirely beleaguered, and General

Townshend, who had at first estimated that he had rations at fullscale for one month for British troops and two months for Indians, urgently asked for his relief to be accomplished not later than the middle of January, because, he said (not realizing that the Turks did not intend to press their attacks), his ammunition would not hold out for many actions like that of the 24th.

On the 28th, the War Committee, which had been holding a series of deliberations on the situation came to the conclusions: that no more divisions could be made available for Mesopotamia because France was the main theatre of war and it was there that maximum strength must be maintained and it was essential to keep an adequate force in Egypt; that after the relief of Kut (which it was assumed would be effected by the forces then in the country) British policy in Mesopotamia was to be purely defensive; and that with this in view defensive positions should be prepared at Qurna and Shaiba. In other words, after the relief of General Townshend, the Expedition was to restrict its activities to enforcing our original policy in Mesopotamia.

The relief of Kut, however, was not the simple problem it appeared, at first, to be. General Nixon was faced with two main alternative courses: either to operate quickly with the troops which he had, or to complete the concentration of all his reinforcements before attempting battle. Unfortunately, the situation in the matter of reinforcements was most unsatisfactory. The arrival of the 3rd and 7th Divisions from France had been very much delayed and the subordinate formations and units of the divisions were arriving piecemeal, because suitable ships for trooping purposes had not been available at Marseilles and because in order to hasten the arrival of the convoy at Basra the troops had not stopped in Egypt for re-organization - as had been intended. The general result was that General Aylmer, who arrived on December 12th from India to take command of the relief-force estimated that the whole corps would not be ready to advance until late January.

General Townshend was urgently demanding relief by the middle of January, which meant that General Aylmer must advance not later than the 3rd. General Nixon, therefore, decided that, although he was most unwilling for the Tigris Corps to advance in detail against an enemy whom he estimated to be considerably its superior in strength, the operations must begin. Accordingly he ordered General Aylmer to advance on the 3rd, with Sheikh Saad as his objective. General Aylmer had succeeded in concentrating the 7th Division, the 6th Cavalry Brigade and certain Corps Troops (16 battalions, 17 squadrons and 42 guns) at Ali Gharbi. Meanwhile, from the eastward movement of Turkish troops, he had deduced that the enemy did not intend to risk another heavy assault on Kut, and therefore, that General Townshend's situation was a little less critical than it had been. Realizing that he had a little more time in hand, he modified his plan to the extent of ordering the 7th Division not to make a decisive attack upon the enemy at Sheikh Saad but merely to pin him to his positions until the remainder of the Tigris Corps could be brought up.

Unfortunately, there was a misunderstanding over this order, with the result that on January 6th the 7th Division attacked at Sheikh Saad with very insufficient artillery support, and by early morning on the 7th found itself irrevocably committed to a serious battle. General Aylmer himself assumed direction of the operations that day, but in the face of an accurate and heavy artillery and rifle fire, handicapped by mirage and by the fact that the sun was in the eyes of the attackers, he was able to make but little ground. At night heavy rain fell, which made movement difficult, and the next day the attack made no progress. That night, too, it was wet; but in the darkness the Turks evacuated part of their position, so that on the 9th General Aylmer was able to advance to Sheikh Saad, the enemy having retired upstream to Ora and Sinn. It was a step towards Kut, but it was one which cost four thousand British casualties out of about eighteen thousand effectives and caused great suffering to the troops.

By now both the 3rd and 7th infantry divisions of the Tigris Corps had arrived, consequently General Aylmer decided that he was in a position to undertake an attack on Hanneh, although he was restricted to making a frontal attack because the floods on the right bank prevented the movement of troops there. He was short of land transport; his supply and transport personnel was less than a quarter of what was required; there was a shortage of artillery ammunition; the reserve ammunition was in barges instead of in the Divisional Ammunition Column; his bridging material was inadequate; his medical equipment was less than a third of what he wanted; and, his whole force lacked staff, organization and cohesion. Nevertheless, he planned to push forward on January 21st with the 7th Division on the left bank, supporting the attack by enfilade fire from such small detachments as he could ferry across the river.

At noon it began to rain, and in a very short while the country was transformed into a sea of mud. Communications broke down and neither horse, foot, nor wheel could move. General Ayhner's casualties were two thousand seven hundred and forty, and the sufferings of the wounded were horrible. Men lay out all night in pitiless, icy rain, dying from exposure because the medical personnel, heroic in its efforts, was hopelessly inadequate to help them. In the morning, many sepoys were found dead without a mark upon them; others were picked up, petrified and sodden with freezing mud. As much as eight days later, men arrived at Amara with wounds that had remained untended to and which were putrefying, gangrenous and full of maggots.

The attack quite definitely had failed, and on the 22nd General Aylmer was compelled to arrange a truce with the enemy to enable him to collect his wounded.

Over the coming months the two additional relief attempts were successfully repulsed by the Turks. Over a four month period, the Tigris Corps had lost twenty-three thousand five hundred, and the Black Watch had forty-eight troops left out of eight hundred and forty. The 43rd Light Infantry was completely wiped out, and all the troops were worn out. Although the British tried to negotiate, and even purchase, a face-saving truce to save the beleaguered garrison, the Turks would not accept anything less than total capitulation.

The British held out against the constant hammering of the Turkish army which surrounded them for one hundred and forty-three days, but eventually Townshend (with the entire Poona Division) surrendered on April, 29th 1916 after running out of food and fearing for the deteriorating condition of his wounded. Overall, "A total of 13,309 personnel surrendered, including 272 British and 204 Indian officers, 2,952 British and 6,988 Indian soldiers, and 3,248 noncombatant troops."[44] The British lost more than 25,000 garrison and relieving forces during the siege. Although the Turks treated Townshend well in captivity, most of the British prisoners were lead on a death march having to walk hundreds of miles into a brutal internment, with over 4,000 dying in captivity.[45] (The British had not surrendered en masse on that scale since the Battle of Yorktown in 1781.)

Captain Robert Palmer died while trying to relieve the British forces at Kut. The battle is described in several letters to his parents by soldiers of his battalion.

1. By an Officer who was there.

> The Turkish position, which is about ten miles up stream from Shaikh Saad, is on the left bank of the Tigris. The position is a very strong one, thoroughly entrenched, with the river protecting its right flank and absolutely secured on its left flank by a very extensive marsh which stretches for miles.
>
> Our camp was about five miles from the Turkish position (down stream) but our forward trenches were within about 1,000 yards of it.

On January 20th our guns bombarded the enemys trenches at intervals during the day, and on the following morning at 3 a.m. we moved out of camp preparatory to the attack which was to commence about 6.30 a.m.

Brigade was to push the main attack with the - brigade (ours) in support of it, whilst a third brigade was to make a holding attack on our right.

The leading brigade entrenched itself during the night within about 500 yards of the position, whilst our Regiment with one Indian Regiment formed the first line of supports. We were in our trenches about 1,000 yards from the enemy s position, ready to make the attack, by 6 a.m.

For some reason, which I do not know, the attack was delayed, and our guns did not open fire till 7.45 a.m. instead of 6.30 as originally intended.

At 7.55 a.m. after our guns had bombarded the enemy's trenches for only ten minutes the infantry were ordered to advance to the attack, our support line advancing at the same time.

Our Battalion, which consisted of three Companies (one Coy being in Kut-el-Amara) advanced in three lines, "B" Coy forming the first line under Lieut. Needham, "C" Coy, the second line under Capt. Page Roberts, and "D" Coy, the third line under Capt. North with Capt. the Hon. R. Palmer as his 2nd in command. Lt. Col. Bowker was with the third line.

As soon as we left the trenches we were under a

heavy rifle fire, and as we advanced this became more and more intense, with machine gun and shrapnel fire added. The ground was perfectly flat and open with no form of cover to be obtained, and our casualties soon became very heavy. We continued to advance till we got to within about 150 yards of the enemy's trenches, but by this time our casualties were so heavy that it was impossible to press home the attack without reinforcements, though at the extreme left of our line, our troops actually got into the first line of trenches, but were bombed out of them again by the Turks.

No reinforcements reached us, however, and we afterwards heard that the Regiment which should have come up in support of us was enfiladed from their right and was consequently drawn off in that direction. All we could do now was to hold on where we were, making what cover we could with our entrenching tools, and this we did until darkness came on, when we withdrew.

The weather had been terrible all that day and night, there being heavy rain with a bitterly cold wind coming off the snow hills. The ground became a sea of mud which made it most difficult to remove the wounded, and many of these had to lie out till the armistice was arranged the following day.

2. By another officer at the battle.

The fighting on the 21st was a pure slaughter. It

was too awful. . .

The troops from France say that in all their experience there they never suffered so much from weather conditions.

We were wet to the skin and there was a bitter wind coming off the snow hills. Many poor fellows died from exposure that night, I am afraid… and many of the wounded were lying out for more than twenty-four hours until the armistice was arranged the following day.

3. Another written from a private's account.

The three Companies of Hampshires were in support, with two native Regiments, and a Battalion of Connaught Rangers. The Black Watch and Seaforths were in the firing line. The Hants men were next the river. The two native Regiments refused to leave their trenches when they saw the fierce fire from the machine guns. The Connaughts were fighting further off. So the Hampshire men were obliged to go on alone. We never made a rush, and just walked slowly through the rain. A slow march to our deaths, I call it.

4. A response to an inquiry by Robert Palmer's parents:

Dear Lady Selborne,

I have just received a letter from 2nd Lt. C. H.

Vernon, recording his search for my son's body on the 7th April, 1916, its discovery (as he believes) and its burial. He also adds that "at the same time he looked for Capt. Palmers, but could not find him. It was afterwards that he heard of his death in the Turkish Camp," and he adds, "Some stories have come through from survivors as to how he lost his life. As far as we can gather, he was the only Hants officer actually to penetrate the Turkish trenches with a few men. That was on the extreme left close to the river. Our men, however, had not been supplied by the Indian Government with bombs. Consequently the Turks, being so provided, bombed them out, and only one or two men escaped capture or death. It was here that Capt. Palmer was mortally wounded while trying to rally his men to hold the captured sector."

5. Another response to an inquiry by Robert Palmer's parents:

Dear Lord Selborne,

About six days ago I went out to the Turks to discuss terms for the surrender of Kut. I spent the night in their camp and have been with them several times since then. I asked them for information about three names. About two of the names I could get little information. On the third day I received a message from

> Ali Jenab Bey, telling me that your son had died in hospital, and that all that could be done for him had been done, and asking me to tell you how deeply he sympathised with you. The next day Ali Jenab and two other Turks came into our camp. One of them, Mohammed Riza, a relation of Jenab Pashas, told me that your son had been brought in after the fight on the 21st, slightly wounded in the shoulder and badly wounded in the chest. He had been well looked after by the Doctors and the Colonel of the Regiment (I could not find out which Regiment) had visited him, and at the Doctors wish sent him some brandy. He did not suffer and the end came after four hours.

There was plenty of blame for what happened in Kut to go around. Strategic decision makers and operational commanders and staff were blamed for maintaining a parsimonious, peacetime obsession with "economy," creating "an indisposition to forward or press demands" regardless of need, and too often in an atmosphere of isolation from front-line realities. They did not even abandon this obsession with economy after the war started, despite the fact that Parliament had already approved funding of the Indian Army's expenses on all overseas missions conducted on behalf of the Empire.[46] Certain operational commanders and staff even squelched those who tried to demand necessary resources.

The disaster at Kut-al-Amara prompted an investigation by the British Parliament. Although the Mesopotamia

Commission, the investigative board convened by Parliament, attempted to lay the majority of the blame on Nixon and the British authorities in India, the main responsibility for this defeat belonged to the Asquith government. Asquith and his Cabinet had oversight of the British administration in India and the authority to shape its structure and actions both in peace and war. The British government, "had contrived a system by which India in peace kept a larger army than was justified by purely Indian reasons" and "there was a fiction that the army was for local purposes only and that since India was a poor country her army was trained, equipped and organized for local purposes."[51] Furthermore, although Nixon and his superiors in India promoted the advance on Baghdad, it was the Dardanelles Committee that ultimately gave the go-ahead in hopes of a victory that would divert attention from the disaster in Gallipoli and other bad news on the Western Front and the Balkans. Similarly, although the advance up to Kut-al-Amara was within the capability of the Tigris (II) Corps, the attack on Baghdad represented a strategic shift in the campaign that required the Home Government to "become morally responsible for ensuring that this front was as well supplied as any other."[52]

Ultimately, Asquith's government failed to provide its forces in Iraq with the strategic guidance, manpower, and material means to achieve victory. However, the Parliamentary run Mesopotamia Commission had minimal criticism of Asquith's coalition led government because they didn't want to discredit the legitimacy of its own government during a time of war.

The Kut disaster forced the government and military to recognize the unique characteristics of the campaign in Iraq. The environmental conditions and the role of Arab irregulars were a significant contrast to the fighting that British soldiers found in France, the Dardanelles, or East Africa during World War I. Similarly, although the enemy and the weather conditions were similar for British units in the Levant, British forces in Iraq did not have the benefit of a mostly cooperative Arab force or shorter supply lines, like British General Edmund Allenby had in Transjordan and Syria.

The government didn't appreciate that during the summer in Iraq, temperatures can reach up to 125 or 130 degrees fahrenheit. Even in the shade, the heat can be stifling, and the cold desert temperatures at night adds to troop misery and sickness. In the Summer 1916, "the excessive heat made military operations impossible. Our [Army in India] troops were exhausted with sickness - fever, dysentery, boils, cholera, jaundice and scurvy."[47] Casualties from the heat sometimes reached epidemic proportions. In the Summer 1916, 111 out of 139 soldiers from the British Highland Light Infantry became heat casualties even before they reached the front.[48] Similarly, heavy rains and floods periodically menaced British forces and their commanders had to either adjust operations or cease them altogether. In mid-November 1914, General Delamain had to stop advancing because heavy rain "rendered the ground so heavy and muddy as practically to preclude any military movements."[49] Inclement weather and flood waters was one of the reasons given for the failed attempts to relieve the beleaguered garrison at Kut-al-Amara.[50]

To remedy the numerous problems in Iraq, Sir William Robertson, the new Chief of the Imperial General Staff in London became ultimately responsible for all tactical and operational decisions in Iraq and he streamlined the chain-of-command. The General Officer Commanding in Iraq reported now only to the Commander-in-Chief for India who answered only to Robertson on day-to-day military matters. In 1916, Asquith also restructured the Dardanelles Committee, limiting its membership to five and renaming it the War Cabinet. The War Cabinet retained oversight of the Iraq campaign through Robertson, along with all other fronts in the war.[53] While the India Office in London and the Viceroy were no longer involved in the daily operations in Iraq, they were still involved in strategic policy for India.

British forces in Iraq quickly assumed a defensive posture and no special importance was attached either to the possession of Kut or to the occupation of Baghdad. This new attitude allowed the Turks to shift troops from Mesopotamia to Persia to fight the Russians.

Meanwhile, matters in the region were going badly. The Turkish army defeated the Russian army under General Saratov in Persia, leaving the Russians exhausted and quite unable to continue operations without a prolonged period of rest and reorganization. Any effective co-operation between the Russians in Persia and the British on the Tigris was no longer possible and the road to Teheran had been opened to Turko-German enterprise, which was regarded with grave apprehension in

India. The possibility of a hostile advance into Persia raised the fears of the Viceroy and his military advisers so much that the Commander-in-Chief considered the idea of carrying out an offensive on the Tigris as a "counter-irritant" to the situation in Persia.

However, as it was still impossible for the Tigris Corps to carry out more than minor operations, General Lake decided that the only reasonable course was to continue to concentrate upon operational reorganization and to complete that before attempting to carry out any important tactical operations.

Men, arms and ammunition, equipment, railway lines, engines and rolling stock, land and river transport were arriving week by week. To deal with this influx of personnel and material it had been necessary to entirely reconstruct the base port, and around Basra twenty miles of raised earthworks had been built in order to reclaim some fifty square miles of swamp and sluggish creek. On the reclaimed ground, reception-camps, hospitals, repair shops and storage dumps were erected; while at the port itself the river was dredged, cranes were being set up, and wharves had been built. Both at the base and along the river banks roads were under construction; while in addition to the light railway in the forward area, two other railway lines were being laid down, one on the Euphrates from Basra to Nasiriyeh, and the other on the Tigris between Qurna and Amara.

At this point, the War Committee decided upon a change in the chief Command of Mesopotamia.

Lieutenant-General Sir S. F. Maude assumed command of the Mesopotamia Expeditionary Force on August 28th, 1918. He was a keen, well-read soldier and a Staff College graduate who had held important staff appointments in peace and had seen war service in Egypt and South Africa. In 1914, he was given a first grade general staff appointment with the III Corps, and subsequently, commanded successively the 14th Infantry Brigade and the 33rd Division in France, and the 13th Division at Gallipoli and in Mesopotamia. His strong, compelling personality; his unlimited capacity for work; his comprehensive grasp of detail; and, his wide knowledge of every branch of staff work fitted him alike for staff or command.

On his arrival with the 13th Division in Mesopotamia he soon grasped the essential challenges ahead of him and said, "...it is a campaign so full of difficulties and complications as can hardly be realized at home." The brilliant achievements of his Division in the last phase of the Kut relief operations, and his pre-eminence as a leader soon singled him out, and although he was the junior Divisional Commander in the Tigris Corps, his appointment as Corps Commander, in succession to General Gorringe, was universally approved. As G.O.C. Tigris Corps he keenly appreciated his difficulties, which he realized at once to be chiefly due to defective operations. On assuming command, which he did at the personal intervention of Sir William Robertson, he determined to complete the reorganization of the whole Expedition before undertaking anything else.

Although Maude didn't believe that his army was ready to undertake any offensive operation, he didn't believe that the Turks could either. The question he had to ask was, would it be better to move - either to advance or to retreat – or stay put and await attack.

The policy of His Majesty's Government was strictly defensive. it had been specifically stated that no importance was attached to the capture of Kut or to the occupation of Baghdad.

But policy did not remain consistent. In India, apprehensions about the status of Persia and Afghanistan and anxieties over the extension of the war eastwards, racked the political and military headquarters. Swayed by the Viceroy's representations, and anxious for any success, the War Committee began to waver towards a semi-offensive policy of attacking the Turks and defeating them before they could concentrate for an offensive. It was thought that such a movement would appear to have the capture of Baghdad as its object, and therefore, would help British prestige.

The chief of the Imperial General Staff informed the War Committee that in October General Maude's effective strength on the Tigris would be approximately fifty-three thousand infantry, four thousand six hundred cavalry and two hundred and twenty-eight guns, and that the General Staff was of the opinion that it was possible for the Turks to concentrate and maintain not more than sixty thousand troops on the Tigris.

Sir William Robertson said that if our policy was strictly defensive, then withdrawal was the soundest and most economical course, but that if our policy was offensive, then the additional expenditure of military resources which would be required to enable General Maude to enforce it would be disproportionate to the political and military advantages which could be gained. "Anything is better than continuing our present difficult, costly and objectiveless plan." He strongly urged a reversion to the original defensive policy because, he said, we could not afford to keep a hundred thousand men in Mesopotamia holding up forty thousand Turks. The force was too small for an offensive and too large for the defensive.

Nevertheless, although their responsible military adviser had expressed himself thus, on September 28th, the War Committee modified the previous instructions which had defined the scope of the operations. On that day, General Maude was informed by the Chief of the Imperial General Staff that "it is the intention of H.M.G. if and when possible to establish, British influence in the Baghdad Vilayet and that he was to continue to improve his communications and to keep his force as far forward as could be done with safety."

Throughout October and November the general condition of the Force improved by leaps and bounds. In October, General Sir Charles Munro visited Mesopotamia on his way to India and, after a very thorough inspection, he reported that in morale and fighting efficiency, the troops left little to be desired, and operationally a great improvement was perceptible. At the end of November, the light railway between Sheikh Saad and Sinn Abtar was working, and the lines between Qurna and Amara, and Basra and Nasiriyeh were reaching completion. The working capacity of these two lines respectively was five thousand and one thousand tons a week, and that capacity would increase as soon as more railway material arrived from India. The river transport, too, had been very considerably augmented and now was sufficient to ensure a steady flow of troops and material to the front. The 7th Cavalry Brigade had arrived; additional artillery units, Lewis guns, enough machine guns for fifteen new machine-gun companies, and fire companies of motor transport were available in the country. The ration strength of the army now amounted to sixty-four thousand eight hundred British, and one hundred and fifty-six thousand Indian personnel, together with seventy-three thousand animals.

As his final step in reorganization, General Maude reconstituted the Tigris Corps. As it had previously existed, it was a clumsy organization consisting of four divisions of infantry, two brigades of cavalry, and other Corps troops. The shortage of trained staff, and the piecemeal arrival of units in the early months of 1916, had led to over-centralization of control, but now General Maude broke up the unwieldy formation. With the object of increasing flexibility, General Maude reconstituted the Tigris Corps into the I and III Army Corps. Another most important addition to the force was extra bridging-equipment and a mobile unit carrying enough material to build five hundred yards of bridge.[54]

The Turkish XVIII Army Corps (45th, 51st, 52nd Divisions) were still occupying the seemingly impregnable defenses around Sannaiyat and the river front as far as Kut. In all, the hostile forces on the Tigris were estimated at seven hundred cavalry, about twenty thousand rifles, and seventy guns. In Baghdad there were some four or five thousand rifles and on the Euphrates there were scattered detachments amounting to approximately two thousand rifles and eight guns.

By the beginning of December, General Maude had a

distinct advantage over the enemy in numbers, in organization and in efficiency. However, any offensive operations had other considerations: the weather, which in December was liable to be wet, and therefore, might seriously impede the movements of troops and transport; the essential need for avoiding heavy casualties; and, for economy in the expenditure of resources. These points were specially impressed upon General Maude by Sir William Robertson, who laid down twenty-five per cent of effectives as being the limit of casualties which could be risked in any operation in Mesopotamia.

On the 10th December, he issued orders for an advance to the Hai. The offensive to re-capture the territory lost to the Turks was about to begin. [55]

His plan was to surprise the enemy by moving at night and to push forward on the right bank to capture the line of the river Hai. On the 13th, the artillery was to pin the enemy to the left bank by bombardment and to create the impression that an attack upon Sunnaiyat was impending. On the right bank, the Cavalry Division would secure a crossing over the Hai at Basrugiyah before daybreak on the 14th, and after crossing the river, push the enemy back along the western bank of the Hai.

This plan was carried out successfully, with the enemy completely surprised by the night march. Maude continued pressing his attacks, forcing the Turks further up the Tigris. By the end of December, as heavy rains immobilized his troops, he had accomplished his original objectives of establishing his army on the Hai river.

For two months General Maude's troops hammered away

at the enemy's defenses, driving them out of their positions and inflicting heavy casualties upon them. At the Hai, at Khadairi bend, at the Salient, the Turks had struggled valiantly but vainly, to stave off defeat; at Dahra, they were swept off the right bank of the Tigris altogether and between Sheikh Saad and Shumran they held not a yard of ground. This time, unlike the previous year, the very elements themselves were against the enemy, for had the rain fallen a few days earlier, the attack would have been held up and the Turks would have gained a sorely-needed respite in which to reorganize their battered defenses.

While General Maude had been wearing down the enemy on the Tigris, events elsewhere had been showing signs of improvement. In the Caucasus, the Russians were planning an offensive against the Turkish Second Army, as well as an advance southwards towards Mosul, Samarra and Baghdad. In north-west Persia, General Saratov, whose force had been considerably increased, was contemplating an advance against the rear of the Turkish XVIII Corps on the Tigris. It seemed, therefore, that when the winter began to wane, and movement in the mountains became possible, the Turks in Mesopotamia would find themselves subjected to a heavy concerted attack from three directions.

While information was received that the Turks were preparing reinforce their troops in Mesopotamia with troops from the Caucasus and north-west Persia, this did not shake General Maude's confidence. Quite apart from the intended Russian offensive, his strategic situation was satisfactory. He had cleared the right bank of the enemy and their strength on the

Tigris front was only about 10,300 rifles and 91 guns, while his own force amounted to 46,000 rifles and 174 guns.

The most brilliant incident of the whole campaign was the crossing of the Tigris River north of Kut in the Shumran Bend. This happened at the end of two months of terrific fighting and after the Turks had been driven entirely from the west bank of the river and had taken up their final strongly defensive position on the Kut peninsula, the scene of the siege, and down the east bank in the maze of trenches on the field of Sunnaiyat, which they had occupied and had been engaged in strengthening for nearly a year. As the General describes it:

> The waterlogged state of the country and a high flood on the Tigris now necessitated a pause, but the time was usefully employed in methodical preparation for the passage of the Tigris at Shumran. Positions for guns and machine-gun crews to support the crossing were selected, approaches and ramps were made, and crews were trained to man the pontoons. In order to keep our intentions concealed it was necessary that most of the details, including the movement of guns, should be carried out under cover of night. Opposite Sunnaiyat, where it was intended to renew the assault, artillery barrages were carried out daily in order to induce the enemy to expect such barrages unaccompanied by an assault as part of the daily routine. Minor diversions were also planned to deceive the enemy as to the point at which it was intended to cross the river.

The crossing of the river was believed to be a wholly impossible thing, so the enemy was struck with astonishment and had no time to concentrate effective resistance. A captured Turkish officer said they had discussed the possibility of such a move, but had decided against such resistance as, "only madmen would attempt it."

The river was in flood and was three hundred and forty yards wide at the point where the bridge was thrown across. This operation being carried out under machine-gun fire which swept ferries and pontoons and inflicted heavy losses on the British. But, in the words of General Maude, the men worked with "unconquerable valor and determination."

As his army crossed to the left bank and put pressure on the Turk's strong defenses at Sunnaiyat, General Maude's plans succeeded better than he could have hoped. At the cost of comparatively few casualties, he had driven the enemy out of the first four lines of the main stronghold; he had secured a position on the left bank from which he could intercept the retreat of the enemy's army, and he had inflicted far heavier casualties than he had received.

At Sunnaiyat, during the night 23rd, the Turkish XVIII Army Corps had rapidly fallen back. By dawn on the 24th, the 7th Division had pushed on to occupy the fifth line of defense and was preparing to advance to the sixth line. At 6:30am, air reconnaissance showed the enemy to be in full retreat. General Maude thereupon issued orders for the 1st Corps to press on, and for the Cavalry Division to cross the river at Shumran and take up the pursuit of the retiring enemy.

Completely demoralized, the Turks streamed away over the desert towards Baghdad, pursued by British warships until darkness compelled a halt. Though, neither the 3rd Corps nor the Cavalry Division attained a decisive success during the day, the intervention of the naval flotilla that prevented the Turk's XVIII Corps from drawing off in comparatively good order, and caused their forces which had so stoutly fought at Sunnaiyat, at Khadairi, at Dahra, practically to cease to exist as an organized body.

On the February 24th, General Maude telegraphed to the Chief of the Imperial General Staff, using almost the exact words used by General Nixon in 1915. He said, "Road to Baghdad seems quite open..." and asked for instructions for his future action.

On February 28th, at Aziziyeh, just half-way to Baghdad, the spot where the original fatal decision was made by General Nixon, General Maude halted for re-concentration and reorganization of his lines of communication. Although anxious to allow his demoralized enemy no respite, and although by pausing he was missing an opportunity to smash the enemy's resistance before it could be re-organized, Maude's operations were not designed to maintain a rapid and prolonged advance. His Chief of Staff and his Q.M.G. advised him that his land transport could not keep his force supplied with all it needed.

On the 2nd March, General Maude received a telegram from the Chief of the Imperial General Staff informing him that, subject to the security of his force and to the capacity of his communications, he was to press on towards Baghdad and exploit his success to the full extent which he himself judged "useful and feasible." The telegram went on to say that the superiority of the British and Russian forces, which would shortly be operating in Mesopotamia, appeared to be sufficient to enable General Maude safely to occupy Baghdad, provided that he felt that he could maintain a force of four divisions of infantry and one of cavalry there, and informed him that the 13th Division would remain at his disposal and that more troops would be sent to him from India for duty on the lengthened line of communication.

Unfortunately, the pause in the operations was used by the enemy, too, who availed themselves of the sorely-needed respite to organize a last attempt to block the road to Baghdad and to effect a junction between the two widely-separated Corps (the XIII and XVIII).

The enemy made a final strong stand in a previously entrenched position at the Diyala River.

On the morning of March 7th, the Turks were found to be holding a position on the right bank of the river on a front of about thirteen miles. Deeming the enemy's force to be nothing more than a rearguard, General Maude ordered the 3rd Corps to force a crossing of the Diyala on the night of the 7th, while he constructed a bridge across the Tigris, ten miles down stream, over which he could pass troops to the right bank to advance direct upon Baghdad.

The Diyala proved to be strongly held by the remnants of the XVIII Corps and for three days the British troops suffered decimating fire from concealed machine-gun batteries as they worked in vain to force a passage over the stream by ferry and pontoon. Eventually about 100 men and four officers from the 6th Loyal North Lancashires established a tiny bridgehead. Fierce Turkish opposition prevented reinforcement and there began an epic battle of endurance under fire.

For over 30 hours the small band fought off attack after attack, often at the point of the bayonet. Finally, on the third night, the East Lancashire's at last succeeded in getting across the Diyalah River to reinforce them. When relieved the small force was down to four officers and 35 men, many of them wounded, and down to the last of the ammunition. Their senior officer, Captain Oswald Austin Reid, King's Regiment attached to the 6th Battalion The Loyal North Lancashire Regiment, was awarded the Victoria Cross.

Meanwhile General Maude, who had taken one of the big paddle-wheel supply-boats for headquarters, moved on up the river and at a point a few miles south of the mouth of the Diyala threw a bridge across and transferred two infantry divisions and his one division of cavalry to the west bank, up which they proceeded to march at a forced pace toward Baghdad.

The Turkish army made another stand at Uxnm at Tubal, putting up strong resistance, but by nightfall, the Turks appreciated the hopelessness of their position.

On both banks of the Tigris the British, in vastly superior numbers, were overwhelming the defenses, and their columns were converging upon Baghdad. To continue to stand outside the city meant the annihilation of the XVIII Corps. On the night of the 10th, the Turks withdrew from the positions covering

Baghdad and retreated northwards up the river.

The British Army entered Baghdad virtually unopposed on March 11, 1917.

It was a matter of considerable regret to most persons concerned that General Maude made no triumphal demonstration upon his arrival at Baghdad. It was thought that a display of pomp and a parade of victory might have a properly subduing effect upon the native population and serve to enhance the local prestige of the conquering forces. But General Maude was undemonstrative in every way. In obedience to his orders a few troops were marched through the city from the south entrance, and a patrol of the streets was instantly established. But as for himself, he ordered the captain of his floating headquarters to bank in at the river wall under the British Residency, and, accompanied only by his personal staff, he walked ashore and up into the city as casually as he might have done had he been only a very tired traveler arriving under the most ordinary circumstances.

Although various British intelligence reports of suspect origin claimed that the Empire planned a counterattack to retake Baghdad, and although at the moment reports of the arrival of Turkish reinforcements in Mesopotamia were vague, it was clear that there was no time to waste in preparing a defense of their position.

General Maude intended, having gained touch with the Russians, to concentrate upon the defeat of the remnants of the XVIII Corps on the Tigris, while the Russians continued to pursue the XIII Corps and to carry out an advance from the

Caucasus upon Mosul. It soon became apparent, however, that this co-operation was not forthcoming.

In Russia, the Revolution had begun, and in the Caucasus and in Persia, their troops were exhausted, short of food, munitions and money. On April 23rd, General Maude was informed that the Russian advance on Mosul would not take place, and that the limit of Russian responsibility could only be the occupation of a line many miles north of Baghdad and Mosul. The general effect of this development in the situation was to leave the British entirely responsible for the security of Baghdad, and of the whole of Mesopotamia as far as the Persian Gulf.

Baghdad was the focus of converging routes, all of which the enemy could advance on, and there was a very real danger that by cutting the "bunds" on the Tigris and the Euphrates the Turks could flood the desert for miles around the city. The only effective way to deal with the situation was to push out beyond Baghdad to occupy defensive positions on the lines of approach, and on positions from which the danger-points on the "bunds" could be made secure.

A Turkish winter offensive against Baghdad was in preparation, and General Maude knew that his enemy was improving communications and forming dumps of ammunition along the banks of the Euphrates. With a view to keeping the counter offensive at arms length, General Maude attacked the Turkish position at Samarrah in April and Ramadi in July. Owing to the unexpected great heat, a dense sandstorm, and the absence of drinking water, this attack failed, and for the moment no further action took place in Mesopotamia.

Meanwhile, the Turks decided to re-focus their energies on Palestine, so as a result, they diverted their reserves from Mesopotamia, and the "Yilderim" army, planned for the recapture of Baghdad, never came within the reach of General Maude, who now found himself virtually free of any threat of attack.

Unfortunately, Maude died of cholera in early November 1917, probably due to tainted milk.

General Sir William Raine Marshall took Maude's place, and subsequently, scaled back operations in Iraq. The next year, Marshall directed the final significant British campaign on the Iraqi front. General Marshall continued north and subsequently captured Tikrit in July 1918 and Kirkuk (it had been previously occupied by the British for a temporary period in May 1918) in October 1918.

The Battle of Sharqat in late October 1918 led to the capture of the northern oilfields near Mosul and the ultimate defeat of Turkish forces in Iraq. During this last battle, the British effectively destroyed the Ottoman 2nd and 5th Divisions and took 11,322 Turkish prisoners.[57] On November 1st, when the head of the British column had reached a point within twelve miles of Mosul, an Armistice with Turkey was declared. Two days later, in accordance with a clause in the terms of the Armistice, British troops entered Mosul, and the Turks evacuated the city on November 10, 1918.[58]

The Mesopotamia Campaign was over. In November 1918, Mesopotamia from Mosul to the Persian Gulf, from the

Kurdish mountains to the Syrian desert was under British sway. Militarily and politically, Turkish influence was destroyed.

Although victorious, the British had invested a large amount of men and material for an area of the world it considered to be a secondary theater of operations - the Western Front being the primary theater. The military suffered over 98,000 casualties, committed over 890,000 total combat and support personnel, yet never faced more than six divisions of Ottoman troops during the entire campaign.[59] Just as Germany had hoped, significant numbers of British troops were drawn away from Western Europe. As General Eric Ludendorff, First Quartermaster General of the German Army (1916-1918), wrote in his memoirs after the war, "The stiffer the Turkish defense in Palestine and Mesopotamia, and the larger the force absorbed in the English effort to achieve their object, the more our burden in the West would be lightened."[60] Similarly, a British soldier of the Expeditionary Force 'D' made the following comment, "We [Army in India soldiers] wished that we were killing Germans, the real menace to civilisation, and not these dupes, Arabs and Turks, whom they had drawn around them in a double coil of protection."[61]

# CHAPTER 10

# THE FIGHTING ENDS BUT THE BATTLE BEGINS

There was no more of a plan to conduct post-conflict operations than there was an operational plan to achieve victory. British intervention in Mesopotamia created a political vacuum once the Turks withdrew, so the British had to decide how it would formulate its future policy in the region.

The two strategic goals the British had sought to complete when Expeditionary Force 'D' first landed on the Fao peninsula in November 1914 - the protection of their oil supplies and the securing of their lines of communication to India - had been met. But these objectives were accomplished at great cost of British manpower, material resources, and prestige. Before the war ended, two significant agreements in 1916 helped shaped postwar events in Iraq. Although they were intended as short-term expedients, they had long-term consequences for Iraq and the Middle East.

The secret Sykes-Picot Agreement of 1916 between the British and French sought to divide up the crumbling Ottoman Empire into areas of direct rule and spheres of influence. Parts of Turkey, Syria, Lebanon, and northern Iraq went to the French, while the rest of Iraq and parts of Saudi Arabia went to the British. Palestine was originally intended to become an international protectorate, although the Britain ruled it as a Mandate after the war. While the British suspected that Mosul had considerable oil production potential at that time, this interest was sacrificed under the assumption (pre-1917 Revolution) that possible Russian expansion would make the city the target for future attack and they wanted the French to bear the brunt of any potential Russian expansion in that area. The British War Office stated, "From a military point of view, the principle of inserting a wedge of French territory between any British zone and the Russian Caucasus would seem in every way desirable."[62]

However, after the Bolshevik Revolution in 1917 and the end of the war in 1918, and prior to the Treaty of Versailles negotiations in January 1919, Lloyd George's government recognized that the Sykes-Picot Agreement hindered their goals in the Middle East. Britain wanted Mosul, for its potential oil reserves, and Palestine as a buffer for the Suez Canal and a homeland for the Jews.

British Prime Minister Lloyd George and French Premier Georges Clemenceau renegotiated the Sykes-Picot Agreement, with the British asking the French to relinquish claims on both Mosul and Palestine. Although no formal notes were taken during the verbal renegotiation (conducted prior to the negotiations of the Treaty of Versailles), it is widely believed that Clemenceau made these concessions based on the assurance that Britain would provide a quid pro quo. "Apparently Clemenceau believed - wrongly, as it turned out - that he had obtained at least the tacit agreement of Lloyd George to support France's claims in Europe in return for Clemenceau's express agreement to grant Britain's claims in the Middle East."[63] Ultimately, this concession afforded Britain additional prestige by its new territorial possessions in the Middle East. However, it should be noted that neither leader apparently pre-coordinated this verbal agreement with their own cabinets, which caused considerable turmoil in the formulation of the foreign policies of their respective countries after World War I.

A second agreement in 1916 had considerable influence on the expectations of many Iraqis. Hussein ibn Ali, an Ottoman vassal and Sharif of Mecca, promised the British that he would lead a revolt against the Turks by Arab officers and Arab supporters in the Ottoman army in exchange for British support of his rule of a post-war independent Arab kingdom. Reeling from the disaster in Gallipoli and desperate for any support that could help defeat the Turks, Sir Arthur McMahon, British High Commissioner in Egypt, promised Sharif Hussein that Britain would support an independent Arab Kingdom if he could successfully produce this revolt.[64] Hussein and his sons (most notably, Amir Feisal) subsequently did lead the June 1916 Arab revolt, marching northward from Arabia with British forces into Transjordan and Syria. Although the revolt did not prompt the massive uprising against the Turks that he had promised, Hussein and his followers expected the British to deliver on their pledge to support Arab independence after the Ottoman Empire disintegrated.

Although the British and French had no intention of meeting these expectations, to convince the U.S. of their commitment to self-determination for the Arab people, France and Britain issued a joint declaration in early November 1918 promising the "complete and definitive liberation of the peoples so long oppressed by the Turks" and "the establishment of indigenous Governments and Administrations in Syria and Mesopotamia."[65] This declaration further raised the expectation among the Iraqi population of self-determination, and the British did find a potential candidate in Amir Feisal Hussein to satisfy their future political requirements. They wanted Feisal, who had already set up a temporary administration in Damascus alongside occupying British troops, to rule Syria.[78]

Thus, these two agreements, along with the Anglo-French declaration, set the foundation for Britain's postwar actions in Iraq, and influenced how the Iraqi people viewed their new foreign occupiers.

While the future of the former Ottoman possessions would mostly be decided at Versailles in 1919, Britain had already began to examine what it would do with the territories it occupied. Foremost in the government's thoughts was the control of Iraq's oil reserves, which provided a cost-effective and politically appealing alternative to importing oil from US and Mexico.[67] However, in addition to the economic benefits, Iraq provided Britain with secure air and land lines of communication to India and a solid footing in the strategically important Middle East.

While outright colonization a was political impossibility thanks to President Wilson's Fourteen Points, which promoted self-determination for former colonies, the burdensome expenses of the war, prompted Britain to seek a compromise that would allow it to enjoy the significant economic and strategic advantages of maintaining a presence in Iraq.[66]

At the end of World War I, Britain's policy in Iraq, and the Middle East as a whole, was exacerbated by a lack of consensus among decision makers in the government. The Arab Bureau favored indirect rule led by a Hashemite monarchy, while the Viceroy and India Office lobbied for direct rule to better protect the periphery of India's borders.[68] The Treasury preferred the cheapest administration possible, regardless of its level of control, and the Eastern Committee, established in 1918 to formulate British policy in the Middle East, could not make up its mind on Iraq even though they supported self-determination for all other Arab areas in the Middle East.[69]

Although the Viceroy and India Office lost control of the Iraq military operation in 1916, they continued to manage the civil administration, which proved to be a considerable challenge. Basra, Baghdad, and Mosul had never been ruled within one single administrative unit because of the distinct geographical, ethnic, and religious characteristics of each. However, due to the administrative advantages of incorporating all of Iraq into one unified entity, the local British authority decided to govern all three vilayets as one. The initial responsibility for Iraq's governance fell to Sir Arnold Wilson, who served as acting civil commissioner from April 1918 to October 1920.[70]

Although President Woodrow Wilson's Fourteen Points had significant influence on policy makers in London, the Viceroy and his subordinates in Iraq were, "cut off from the post-war European turmoil and insulated from the effects of Wilson's liberal rhetoric,"[71] and they wanted to impose direct rule in Iraq.

A proponent of the British imperial style of rule, Sir Arnold Wilson believed that the diverse Iraqi population would not be able to unify and cooperate sufficiently to rule themselves. He believed that to "install a real Arab Government in Mesopotamia is impossible, and, if we attempt it, we shall abandon the Middle East to anarchy."[72] Furthermore, after the Anglo-French declaration in November 1918, he told the India Office that, "the country as a whole neither expects nor desires any such sweeping scheme of independence."[73] Wilson primarily argued that Britain should govern Iraq until it was ready to rule itself because "efficient, benign government was of far more benefit to the people than anarchical independence."[74]

The assumption of British control of the three former vilayets during and after World War I prompted varying reactions among the ethnic and political elites in Iraq. Although the majority of the population welcomed the removal of the Ottoman administration, they were wary of British intentions. As the British occupied Najaf and Karbala late in the war, Iraqi leaders, Shia clerics, and tribal sheikhs formed the Jamiyya al-Nahda al-Islamiyya (Society of Islamic Revival), whose purpose was to defend Islam against the British and the tight controls imposed by the military occupation. Their opposition resulted in the assassination of a British official in spring 1918, which prompted the British blockade of Najaf and the imposition of other punitive measures.[75] Sunni Iraqis formed an opposition group as well. A group of ex-Ottoman officers who fought with Amir Feisal during the Arab Revolt in 1916, formed the al-Ahd al-Iraqi (The Iraqi Covenant) in 1918, and a predominately Shia-based opposition group, the Haras al-Istiqlal (Independence Guard), formed in 1919. Both of these groups believed in an independent Iraq led by a Hashemite ruler.[76] Likewise, although the Kurds in the north initially welcomed the British, Wilson's administration eventually clashed with various Kurdish leaders as well. Together, these groups provided the foundation and leadership for the eventual opposition to British rule in Iraq.

Not all in Wilson's administration in Iraq believed in direct rule. Gertrude Bell, Oriental secretary and key Wilson advisor, initially supported Wilson's position but later concluded that direct rule would not likely succeed. The strength of the contemporary nationalist movements in Egypt, Syria, and India led her to promote limited self-rule in Iraq with British oversight. To establish this type of government, she believed that the "British should work with the largely urban and Sunni nationalists to modernize the country and to end what she regarded as the reactionary and obscurantist influence of Shia clerics and their tribal followings."[77] She, therefore, tried to work closely with the ex-Ottoman officers who served with Amir Feisal during the Arab Revolt to help realize her vision for the future of Iraq.

As the negotiations of the Treaty of Versailles began, France maintained its desire to acquire Syria. Although Clemenceau waived French claim to Mosul (thanks to oil concessions by the British) and Palestine, he drew the line on Syria since the French had historical and commercial interests there. Frenchmen had fought along side Christian Maronites during the Crusades and "had historically been the protector of the Christian communities throughout the Ottoman Empire."[79] French business interests in Lyon desired Syrian silk, and most importantly, Clemenceau knew French public opinion would be outraged if he relinquished Syria to the British.[80] The French population had suffered greatly in the war and wanted a share of the spoils, but when the Treaty of Versailles was signed in June 1919, there was no formal decision on Syria's final status.

After several months of contentious debate between France and Britain, Lloyd George turned his back on his government's promise of an independent Arab Kingdom and bowed to Clemenceau's demands for Syria because of: his fear of further alienating France; the increasingly nationalist character of Feisal's administration in Damascus (Syria's Congress proclaimed him King in March 1920); and the expenditure involved in maintaining a garrison in Damascus.[81] In April 1920, Britain and France signed the San Remo Treaty confirming Britain's control over Iraq and Palestine (which included Transjordan), and France's control over Syria (which included Lebanon).

All of these territories were governed under a League of Nations Mandate "A" Class, which called for eventual independence of each country within twenty-five years. Britain's responsibility was to ensure that Iraq would eventually satisfy the four criteria of internationally sanctioned sovereignty: (1) that the state be capable of maintaining its territorial integrity and political independence, (2) that it be able to maintain the public peace throughout the whole territory, (3) that it have adequate financial resources to provide regularly for normal

Government requirements, and (4) that it have laws that afforded equal and regular justice for all.[82]

Although France and Feisal negotiated the future of their relationship, they could not reach an accommodation. In the Bekaa Valley, Arab irregulars harassed the French by sniping at their troops, and there were clashes with French troops in other parts of Lebanon as well. In July 1920, the French sent Feisal an ultimatum to accept the Mandate and to punish those who had attacked French forces, but Feisal refused and the French unceremoniously evicted his administration from Syria in late July.[83]

Most Iraqis viewed the Mandate as an annexation and a betrayal of Britain's wartime promises of self-determination, and trouble soon followed. Shia clerics, tribal sheiks, and former Ottoman bureaucrats all feared for their overall standing under this Mandate and rapidly established organized opposition to British rule. In March 1920, the al-Ahd al-Iraqi in Syria "declared the independence of Iraq under the kingship of Amir Abdallah, brother of Amir Feisal."[84] In April, Ayatollah Muhammad Taqi al-Shirazai issued a fatwa in Karbala "declaring that service in the administration was unlawful."[85] In May, members of the al-Ahd al-Iraqi marched from Syria into Iraq and captured Tall Afar. They then began a march on Mosul with the intention of fomenting a revolt, however, the British dispersed their forces before they arrived and the revolt never took place.[86] At the end of June, al-Shirazai issued another fatwa, seeming to promote armed conflict.

In an attempt to preempt any rebellion, the British

detained several tribal chiefs in the mid-Euphrates region, but these arrests had the opposite effect. Revolt soon took hold in the mid-Euphrates and spread from Karbala and Najaf to the lower Euphrates and most of Baghdad as well. Uprisings also took place in southern Kurdistan.[87] A significant feature of this rebellion was the remarkable cooperation between the Shia and Sunni communities, with both using mosques to promote anti-British agitation.[88] The Haras al-Istiqlal, who had close ties to al-Shirazai, acted as a link between the Shia and Sunni Arab communities that sought independence.[89]

By July, Iraq was in full-blown revolt. There were approximately 130,000 rebels, of which 59,000 had rifles.[90] The British had only 29,500 combat soldiers suited for quelling this rebellion and they were scattered across the entire country.[91] To augment the British land forces, the Royal Air Force provided two squadrons of light bombers and the Royal Navy still had eight 100 ton armed vessels left over from the war.[92] In Rumaitha (150 miles south of Baghdad), rebels attacked government buildings, besieged the British garrison, cut the railway, and blocked reinforcements. The situation in northern Iraq became so tenuous for the British that General Aylmer Haldane, General Officer Commanding of British forces in Iraq, asked his military chain-of-command in London permission to use gas artillery shells.[93] While that request was denied, the British did dispatch ground reinforcements from Iran and India.[94] Overall, the Royal Air Force played a significant role in support of ground troops by logging 4,000 flying hours and dropping 100 tons of bombs. It lost eleven aircraft and fifty-seven were damaged.[95]

The rebellion eventually lost steam. Tribal sheiks in Kut-al-Amara and Amara did not participate in the revolt for fear of jeopardizing their British-granted landholdings, and Basra merchants did not want to support the revolt for fear of endangering their extensive business ties with the British. Furthermore, the rebels geographical separation allowed the modernly equipped British forces to regroup and counterattack, eventually reasserting control.[96] By October, the rebellion was mostly over after the relief of Rumaitha and the surrender of Karbala and Najaf.

By the end of rebellion, the British suffered 450 soldiers killed (both British and Indian), 450 missing, and approximately 1,100 wounded,[97] while approximately 6,000 Iraqis died in the conflict.[98] In monetary terms, the cost of the rebellion to Britain was forty million pounds sterling.[99] The biggest losers of the rebellion were Wilson and the Shias. This rebellion discredited Wilson's support of direct rule and ensured his eventual replacement, and the Shias lost significant influence in the development of Iraq's future because the British viewed the Shia mujtahids (religious scholars) as being one of the main instigators of this revolt.[101]

From a counterinsurgency perspective, the British drew from experiences ranging from the Indian frontier wars to the Boer War to quell the revolt. Haldane's conduct of operations mirrored instructions articulated in British General C.E. Callwell's Small Wars (first published in 1896), the definitive work of nineteenth century British counter-insurgency doctrine. The revolt demonstrated both that cavalry could still play a role against a lightly armed foe in a desolate environment, as well as the value of using armored cars in conjunction with infantry forces. The uprising also showed the limitations of aircraft against irregular forces and the overall limited capabilities of the Army in India outside the subcontinent.[102]

The cost of suppressing the rebellion motivated the British government to allow the Iraqis to take a more active role in governing their own country, albeit with substantial British influence. As a result of the rebellion, the British increased the total number of troops to 102,000 soldiers (17,000 British and 85,000 Indians), which cost an estimated thirty million pounds sterling annually.[103] Overall, the British sought to maintain its Mandates in the Middle East by allowing more self-determination, subsidizing select Arab rulers (e.g., Ibn-Saud of the Arabian Peninsula, the Iman of Yemen, etc.), and providing a security presence primarily through the Royal Air Force, which they believed to be a low-cost alternative to stationing large numbers of ground forces.[104]

Sir Percy Cox replaced Wilson in October as the High Commissioner under the new Mandate, however, even without the rebellion, Wilson would have been replaced due to his insistence on direct rule, which was in conflict with the pre-revolt preferences of the Eastern Committee and the Foreign Office.[105] In November, Cox selected Sayyid Abd al-Rahman al-Kailani, Naqib (a Sunni religious leader) of Baghdad, as the president of an interim council of ministers working under British oversight. This council consisted of twenty-one Iraqi notables (mostly Sunnis, but some Shias, Christians, and one

Jew) from all three vilayets. Although democratic in appearance, the British appointed members of this council who they thought would support their interests.[106] The majority of the Iraqi administration was predominately Sunni, because the British sought to draw upon their experience gained from the former Ottoman administration. The Shias were mostly left out of the new government because they had little administrative skill (due to the discriminatory practices of the Sunni dominated Ottoman administration) and the British thought they lacked reliability due to their role in the rebellion.[107]

After the creation of this short-term government, the India Office and the Viceroy lost the control of the civil administration in Iraq, and the newly created Middle East Department of the Colonial Office assumed oversight of the Mandate. Winston Churchill, as the recently appointed Colonial Secretary, convened the Cairo Conference in March 1921 to organize the future policy of Britain's Mandates in the Middle East. In Cairo, Churchill decided to establish a monarchy led by Amir Feisal and a joint defense composed of an Iraqi Army, the Royal Air Force, and British-led Levies.[108] The British thought the Iraqis would view Feisal favorably due to his Sharifian lineage and his leadership during the Arab Revolt in 1916. They also thought he would have no significant opposition (the British deported his only potential rival, Sayyid Talib of Basra) and would be agreeable to British direction.[109] Additionally, they tried to legitimize Feisal's installation by holding a phony plebiscite in Iraq, in which 96 percent of the population supported his rule.[110]

Feisal's government had significant limitations. He ruled

a country that was not Sovereign; both Shias and Kurds alike distrusted him due to his Sunni heritage; and most significantly, the majority of Iraqis doubted his trustworthiness because of his past association with the British. In general, Feisal had two major challenges to overcome if he was to succeed and maintain power: securing the gradual independence of Iraq and the integration of a diverse country that had never been governed before as a single administrative unit.[111] To buttress his support within the country, Feisal filled the high offices of his government with many of the ex-Sharifian officers who fought with him during the Arab Revolt in 1916 and served with his temporary government in Syria. Many of these officers were Ottoman educated Iraqis who "soon achieved a position in Iraqi politics second only to that of the British and Feisal."[112] Overall, Feisal's administration used a patronage system to maintain both its power and stability in tribal areas.

To give the appearance of an equal arrangement between two independent nations, the British sought to have their relationship with Iraq defined through a treaty. While they viewed this as an opportunity to confirm the Mandate, the majority of the Iraqi population opposed the treaty, especially the Shia population, which viewed this as a consolidation of "a [Sunni dominated] state over which they had no control and which might habitually ignore their interests."[113] Even Feisal opposed this treaty because it made him appear to be a puppet of British domination over the country. He discreetly encouraged anti-treaty opposition, which prompted Abd al-Rahman to resign. During a period in which Feisal suffered appendicitis and had to temporarily abdicate his power, Cox took advantage of the power vacuum and imposed direct rule over Iraq. With no major Iraqi leader to impede him, Cox suppressed radical newspapers and political parties, banished multiple opposition politicians, and bombed tribal insurgents in the mid-Euphrates.

In September, Feisal returned and restored Abd al-Rahman to his former position. Seeing no viable alternative, he signed the treaty with the British in October.[114] The Anglo-Iraqi treaty, which was to last twenty years, gave the British control of Iraq's foreign, security, and financial policy. The British also required Iraq to pay half of its residency requirements, "which not only placed Iraq in a state of economic dependence on Britain but helped retard its development."[115] The treaty also dictated that the Iraqis appoint British officials in eighteen governmental posts to serve as advisors and inspectors. Although this treaty gave the Iraqis highly visible positions of responsibility, the British had the final say in nearly every major aspect of the government. In return, Britain promised to provide military aid and to help Iraq satisfy the League of Nations' requirements for Mandates to earn independence.[116]

Article From: THE LITERARY DIGEST
December 16, 1922

## BRITAIN'S MESOPOTAMIAN BURDEN AND OIL

London newspapers remind us that a Treaty between Great Britain and Mesopotamia, or the Kingdom of Irak, was signed on October 10th at Bagdad, by which, according to the melancholy view of *The Times*, "the Government have linked up the fortunes of the British Empire with all the uncertainties of Mesopotamia for twenty years to come," and it recalls that:

"In the vicissitudes of the war it so happened that British arms detached this territory from Turkey. Thousands of British lives were lost in the effort and British treasure was freely spent in those deserts for a purpose that the struggle in Gallipoli failed to achieve. At the end of the war we found Irak upon our hands, and our Government agreed to accept a mandate for the administration of this inhospitable territory. What relation Irak has to British Imperial interests, whether strategic or economic, no statesman has yet made plain. The strongest argument used for all the continuance of our connection with the country is that, since we have expended such energy in the effort to wrest the country from the Turk and to retain our control, it would be a confession of weakness if we were to relax the strain. The task since the Armistice has been wholly ungrateful. The population rebelled and the rebellion was crusht at great cost. More recently our Government have tried to act on the assumption that the people of Mesopotamia were, or could be made, a definite and coherent nationality. Since their speech is Arabic, they were given an Arab King from the family of the Sherif of Mecca, and the person of the King has been regarded as a possible nucleus of stable government. The King was provided with a Cabinet, and Mesopotamia, with its vague frontiers and mixed population, was treated as a nation, as an embryo State, to be ranked with the modern democracies included under the League of Nations."

"The Treaty is an evasion of the facts. The reason for the conclusion or a Treaty was that the politicians of Bagdad objected to the idea of a mandate, and traded on popular ignorance by objecting to a novel Arabic term. Our Government, therefore, considered themselves obliged to incorporate the normal provisions of a mandate in a Treaty recognizing the independence of Irak. By this Treaty, however, the British Empire undertakes many and serious obligations toward Mesopotamia, besides considerable obligations toward the League of Nations. The obligations of financial and military aid

> are on our side; on the side of King Feisal there is little more than an obligation to accept our advice and to refrain from accepting foreign advisers without our consent. The Treaty is unfair to the British Empire, which has always willingly undertaken an intelligible task, but shrinks from indefinable commitments. It is unfair to the League of Nations, which, in its present experimental stage should not be saddled with a burden that the British Empire can hardly bear."

In the Fall of 1922, the Chanak crisis in the eastern Dardanelles led to the end of the Lloyd George government and a significant policy change toward Iraq. Turkish military forces surrounded British military forces in the Chanak neutral zone because of the British government's policy of supporting Greece against Turkey. Italy and France refused to help the British for fear of being dragged into another conflict, prompting Churchill to declare that the British Empire would be reinforcing Chanak.[117] However, Churchill's declaration was not coordinated with Lloyd George or the rest of his Cabinet, and it was viewed negatively by a British public still waiting for the peace dividend after World War I.

Critical of his foreign policy, Conservative party candidate for Prime Minister, Bonar Law, rebuked Lloyd George for his overseas commitments and accused him of imperial overreach. He stated that "we cannot alone act as the policeman of the world," a sentiment that resonated with the British public.[118] Law and other prospective Members of Parliament (MP) promoted the reduction of British forces in Iraq as a part of their election campaigns. The Chanak crisis rallied the public to the Conservative party and they won the election in November 1922, with Bonar Law becoming Prime Minister.[119]

In December 1922, Law established a committee to decide what to do about Iraq. Parliament seriously discussed evacuating Iraq and Sir Percy Cox was recalled to London to testify before the committee, where he argued that British "policy in Iraq was working, would bear dividends great enough to justify its continuance, and that, if prematurely curtailed, the result would be disastrous."[120] He also stated that a withdrawal "would lead inevitably to anarchy, a rise in Russian influence and ultimately the return of the Turks."[121] Cox's testimony prevented a complete British withdrawal, but the Chanak crisis prompted the Law government to reduce the twenty-year Anglo-Iraqi treaty commitment in Iraq to "a period of four years after a peace treaty had been signed with Turkey."[122]

The final component of building the Iraqi nation-state took place with the Constituent Assembly. The Constituent Assembly ratified the Organic (which embodied the constitution) and Electoral Laws in March 1924. The constitution was a compromise between the requirement of a strong executive and the need to give influential sections of the emerging Iraqi polity (most notably, the sheikhs) a "stake in the new order."[123] The constitution gave the king the power to delay or dissolve parliament, to pick the prime minister, and to choose his ministers on the basis of the prime minister's recommendation. Every law needed his confirmation and he could issue executive ordinances concerning finance, security, and the execution of the term of the treaty with the British when parliament was not in session. The parliament was composed of a senate, whose members were chosen by the king, and an elected chamber of deputies. Additionally, the cabinet "was responsible to the chamber of deputies and the chamber could force the government's resignation by a simple majority vote on a motion of no confidence."[124]

The election law divided the country into three electoral districts and provided for a two-step indirect election. Primary electors were male taxpayers twenty-one and older who elected secondary electors (1 for every 250 voters). The secondary electors had to live in one of the three electoral districts. Once elected, these secondary electors voted in their district headquarters for the individual whom they wanted to serve in the chamber of deputies. Unfortunately for the democratic process in Iraq, both "the large districts and the two-step process allowed for considerable government intervention in the election process, which successive government were not slow to implement."[125]

The constitution became the law of the land and endured with a few modifications until the monarchy was overthrown in 1958. The King became an instrument the High Commissioner used to ensure British interests and the British also ensured the sheikhs, whom they had done much to empower, had a large parliamentary membership. Not surprisingly, the constitution failed to gain legitimacy with the majority of Iraqis "partly because Iraqis were never given real responsibility in the government and partly because they came to regard it as an instrument of foreign manipulation and control."[126]

Although the Anglo-Iraqi treaty and Constituent Assembly helped define the internal government, the Iraqis needed an army to maintain stability and protect its borders. Not only did the nascent country still lack internal unity, but it also had external threats from Turkish irregulars, Kurdish tribesmen, and Wahhabi incursions.[127] Jaafar Pasha al-Askari, an ex-Ottoman officer, served as the first Minister of Defense and helped form the Iraqi Army. In 1922, the Iraqi Army commissioned 250 ex-Ottoman officers and had a total of 3,500 soldiers. Although nominally independent, the Iraqi Army was organized, trained, and equipped along the British model.[128]

In October 1922, to assist the Iraqi Army, the British established an air control system in which the RAF provided the majority of security, augmented by a land force of British officered Levies. The British hoped that this system would be cheaper than garrisoning large numbers of ground troops in Iraq.[129] The first Air Officer Commanding was John Salmond who led "eight squadrons of aircraft, nine battalions of British and Indian infantry, besides local Levies, armoured cars, pack artillery, and supporting units."[130] Sir Henry Dobbs believed this arrangement would provide the majority of Iraq's internal and external defense because he "did not visualize the possibility of Iraq alone ever being able to defend herself against external aggression, and favoured a limited role [for the Iraqi Army]."[131]

The British-led Levies represented a key component of

this air scheme. The Levies were a gendarmerie type force, which traced its origins to a small group of Arab Scouts in Nasiriya that the British used to collect intelligence on the Turks. During World War I, this mostly Arab unit also provided reconnaissance and escort functions for the British military and civil administration. In October 1918, the Levies were formally organized under one command consisting of two branches: a Striking Force in each administrative area to serve as an armed reserve and a District Police subordinate to each political officer. The total forces consisted of 5,467 mounted and dismounted personnel. The Levies chiefly functioned as an internal security apparatus where they served "the executive needs of the Civil Administration."[132]

In August 1919, the Levies were reorganized again. They were divided into three Area Headquarters in Mosul, Baghdad, and Hillah, and expanded their ranks to include ethnic Kurdish and Turkomen personnel. Christian Assyrians were also incorporated in April 1921. Organizationally, mounted units consisted of 100-man squadrons and 25-man troops while the dismounted units had 100-man companies and 25-man platoons.[133] In November 1919, the British formally declared that the Levies would be trained to conduct "rapid advances, flank attacks, advanced and rear-guard action, and marsh fighting. For work in the river areas, work with aeroplanes, armoured cars, and gun boats. They also trained for mountain warfare for the northern areas and for desert warfare anywhere west of Iraq."[134] The British principally attempted to mold the Levies into a multifunctional, native force unit capable of conducting operations in a combined arms environment.

The establishment of the Iraq Army in 1921 prompted the British to limit Levy recruitment only to Assyrians, and Arab or Kurd volunteers were required to enlist in the army. The British chose the Assyrians, first, because of their superior fighting qualities, and secondly, because they didn't trust the Arabs and Kurds.[135] There were problems with this arrangement since most Iraqis resented the Assyrians because of their unwillingness to assimilate, and at the same time, their subservient relationship with the British. Not only did the Iraqi politicians view the Assyrian relationship with the British as an attempt to promote dependence on the British, but the Iraqi Army "saw them [the Assyrians] as an insult to unity and independence."[136]

The Levies participated in multiple operations throughout the country from 1918-1923 to help quell threats to the British and the new Iraqi government. In 1919, the Levies participated in British operations against Kurdish Sheikh Mahmud al-Barzinjah, which ultimately resulted in his capture. In 1920, they stayed loyal to the British and helped restore order during the revolt, even though they were under great pressure from their fellow Iraqis to change sides. During the revolt, seventy-three Levies lost their lives and they were awarded fifteen medals for gallantry.[137] In 1921-23 the Levies conducted multiple operations against various Kurdish factions and in 1922-23, defensive operations to deter Turkish aggression.[138] The Levies were fully integrated in Britain's combined armed operations in Iraq, they "seldom took the field without close support from bombing and fighter aircraft."[139]

The RAF represented the primary element of the British plan to guarantee internal and external order in Iraq, deploying aircraft against reluctant taxpayers, uncooperative tribes, and foreign forces (e.g., Wahabbis) that threatened Iraqi territorial sovereignty.[140] In an era of rapidly declining defense budgets and domestic pressure to downsize its overseas commitments, the British used the RAF because it was a cheap, asymmetrical method of accomplishing its goals, and RAF aircraft were mobile and practically invulnerable to tribesmen whom were usually only armed with rifles.[141]

The RAF's first bombing took place in late 1923 when Sheikhs Kashan al Jazi of Barkat and Azzarah Majun of Sufran failed to pay back taxes and didn't turn in 300 rifles per tribe as a penalty for late payment. The RAF indiscriminately bombed Bakrat and Sufran for two days and nights with incendiary bombs, killing approximately 100 men, women, and children and many horses, cows, and sheep. The bombing prompted the sheikhs to pay the taxes, which was mostly borrowed money, but few weapons were turned in.[142]

The British also used the RAF throughout the Mandate against other recalcitrant tribes in the mid-Euphrates and Kurdish areas. Although an effective means of collecting taxes, quelling tribal revolts, and maintaining territorial sovereignty, the indiscriminate RAF bombing had long-term consequences. Instead of encouraging cooperation and helping maintain social cohesion, the bombing forced many tribe members in Barkat and Sufran to resettle into other tribes not under threat. This migration disrupted national integration and did nothing to encourage the handover of weapons. Similarly, Peter Slugget, a Middle East historian stated, "perhaps the most serious long-term consequence of the ready availability of air control was that it developed into a substitute for administration. Several incidents during the Mandate period indicate that the speed and simplicity of air attack was preferred to the more time-consuming and painstaking investigation of grievances and disputes."[143] Overall, although the RAF served the guarantor of internal and external order, the bombing terrorized the populace and did little to endear individual Iraqis to the British or their central government.

In addition to the bombings, the British used other brutal means of quelling dissent and punishing armed resistance, such as: fines, bribery, deportations, selective arrests, capital punishment, confiscation of property, show of force operations, blockades, and the severing of the water supply to targeted cities. In early 1918, the British imposed a fine of 50,000 Rupees and 500 rifles on a local sheikh in Najaf after he incited a mob to ransack British offices and fire on RAF aircraft. The British eventually cut off the water supply to Najaf until the rifles were handed over and confiscated the sheikh's house in lieu of the fine.[144] During the siege at Kut-al-Amara in 1915-6, the British also shot twelve looters to discourage this activity in the future.[145]

In 1923, Britain and Iraq agreed that Iraq would be responsible for its own defense, allocating 25 percent of its budget to defense, while British assistance would be gradually reduced. Despite the Iraqi Army's nominal autonomy, the British identified its requirements and finances, trained and armed its forces, and monitored operations via "joint consultation." As with the civil administration, this arrangement translated into outright control by the British.[147]

Another obstacle to the integration of the three vilayets into the new Iraqi state was the status of the Kurds, who comprised the majority of the population in Mosul. The Kurds were a different ethnicity than their fellow Arab Iraqis and they spoke their own language. Due to their unique ethnicity and culture, the Kurds have always sought autonomy so that they could handle their own affairs and retain their national identity. Following the disintegration of the Ottoman Empire, the victorious Allies initially promised the Kurds autonomy in the Treaty of Sevres in 1920, which also "stipulated that the Kurds of Turkey and Iraq could apply for admission to the League of Nations within a year."[148] Unfortunately, Mustafa Kamal's emergence in Turkey effectively canceled this treaty after he secured control of the Kurdish areas in the eastern part of his country.

The British had attempted to establish an autonomous Kurdish area in Mosul as early as 1918, appointing Mahmud, who had both extensive landholdings and a recognized political standing, to rule this area. He eventually alienated the British by attempting to become a legitimately independent ruler, and the British subsequently removed him from power in May 1920.[149] However, Kamal's claim on Mosul and the Turkish military's forays in the vilayet in 1922 prompted the British to reinstall Mahmud "to re-establish some kind of authority in the region which would act as a bulwark against further Turkish encroachment."[150] However, Mahmud seized this opportunity to, once again, establish an independent state and the British evicted him from Sulaimaniyya in July 1924 for collaborating with the Turks.[151] Mahmud fled to Persia and conducted a guerrilla war against the British and Iraqi government until his capture in 1931.[152]

In the summer of 1923, the Iraqi government guaranteed that "Kurds would be appointed in Kurdish areas and that the Kurdish language would be employed in Kurdish territory, and it instructed officials to proceed with the elections in all Kurdish areas under their control." This declaration represented the Kurds' formal integration into Iraq, and by 1924, the Kurds dispatched delegates to the Constituent Assembly in Baghdad.[153] As for Turkey's claim on northern Iraq, the Allies and Turkey signed the Treaty of Lausanne in 1923, which settled Turkey's postwar boundaries, but left the final determination of Mosul up to the League of Nations. In July 1925, a League of Nation's commission recommended that Mosul remain in Iraq and that the Iraqi government should allow the Kurds to govern themselves "to develop their cultural identity through their own institutions."[154] This recommendation prompted the Turks to drop all formal claims on Mosul and allowed the British and the Iraqi government to settle the Kurdish question for the time being. The border between Turkey and Iraq was demarcated in 1926.

The formation of the Iraqi state primarily served Britain's interests. The British cobbled three disparate vilayets together to take full advantage of Iraq's strategic and economic potential. To ensure this contrived nation remained intact and continued to do its bidding, the British installed a ruler they could influence; formulated a national-level governmental structure to ensure its dominance; established a security apparatus dependent on its support; and placed its own officials in all levels of the government to make sure that the Iraqis did their will. Not surprisingly, the majority of the Iraqi Army's officer corps (nearly all ex-Ottoman trained) and their Iraqi counterparts in the civil administration resented the al-Wad al-Shadh, or "the perplexing predicament which gave an outward appearance of self-rule whilst preserving the essence over state and army alike."[155]

# CHAPTER 11

# MANAGEMENT OF THE CIVIL ADMINISTRATION

When the Army in India's Expeditionary Force 'D' landed in Iraq in November 1914, British authorities had very little empirical knowledge of the three vilayets. Although many British civil servants and military officers based in India had served in the Persian Gulf sometime in their careers and even spoke fluent Arabic, most were not familiar with the cultural and social realities in the vilayets,[156] so they tried to fill this void by drawing on their past colonial experiences in India and elsewhere.

Some of this knowledge proved valuable for the British, such as the importance of rapidly establishing rapport with local residents and the tolerance of some local customs. However, the misapplication of these experiences, especially in terms of land policy and the administration of justice, had negative long-term effects on Iraq and the British occupation itself.[157]

Britain's efforts to establish a civil administration began with the capture of Basra on November 23, 1914. Although British authorities had no orders to create a permanent administration in Iraq, many British soldiers and civil servants assumed that Britain would eventually annex Basra due to its strategic significance.[158] Sir Percy Cox, chief political officer of Expeditionary Force 'D' declared to the local Iraqi population:

> Let it be known to all that the British Government has had many millions of Mahomedan subjects, more than any other power in the world – more even than Turkey.
>
> The British government has now occupied Basra, but though a state of war with the Ottoman Government still prevails, yet we have no enmity or ill-will against the population, to whom we hope to prove good friends and protectors. No remnant of Turkish administration now remains in this region. In place thereof the British flag has been established – under which you will enjoy the benefits of liberty and justice, both in regard to your religious and your secular affairs.
>
> I have given strict orders to my victorious troops that in the execution of the duties entrusted to them, they are to deal with the populace generally with complete consideration and friendliness. It remains for you yourselves to treat them in the same way.
>
> In conclusion, you are at full liberty to pursue your vocations as usual and your business as before, and it my confident hope that the commerce of Basra will resume its course and prosper even more than in the past.[159]

To make sure the Arabs were in no doubt about British policy, a letter was written to the Arab chiefs:

> You, the Sheikhs of the Arabs, are wise men and

> will not be misled, but some of your ignorant tribesmen may be. It is therefore considered expedient to remind you of the following facts, which are patent to all and cannot be denied.
>
> Great Britain never came into this war willingly. The war was forced upon her simply by the intrigues of Germany, who for her own purposes incited Turkey to commit repeated acts of hostility towards England, so that she might be involved in war with her.
>
> Immediately on the arrival of British forces in Shatt-al-Arab we proclaimed that the British Government had no quarrel with the tribes of Iraq and no designs against their religion … and that the British forces would not attack or molest the Arabs, so long as they maintained a neutral attitude.[160]

General Barrett appointed Major D'Arcy Brownlow, Deputy Judge Advocate-General of the 6th Division, as military commandant for Basra and he had the authority to develop a civil administration without interference from local military commanders.[161]

The very first British action upon entering Basra was to establish "public order" in the city. The Turkish police chief and his staff were gone, and looters had sacked the city. "Forty-eight hours after the Turks had left, not a single government building outside Basra possessed doors or window-frames."[162] Similarly, piracy on the Shatt-al-Arab had resumed and armed bands of criminals operated in the date groves from Basra to Fao.

Reacting to this rise in criminality, the British Provost-Marshal deployed a police force primarily staffed by Indians, who were mostly Punjabi Muslims. The Indian police officers operated effectively and they possessed an ability to quickly learn and speak the Arabic language.[166] They successfully established civil peace by April 1915 their urban patrols to were extended to Amara a few weeks later, then Naziriya.[163] Upon occupying Baghdad, the British conducted house-to-house searches for weapons and prioritized occupation of road connections and bridges.[164]

The British supplemented military police and troops with two forces. Local headmen formed small patrols in the smaller towns. The British recruited an irregular, district police to patrol the hinterlands. These district police proved highly successful, relieving the Army of the need to provide many road and river patrols.[165]

Although many Basra residents were accustomed to working with the British because of economic relationships originating with the East India Company, the establishment of a civil administration was complicated by the lack of official records. The Turkish civil administration, which was rife with corruption and inefficiency, took as many official records as they could with them when they fled Basra.[167] Complicating the administration's problems, many Iraqis were afraid to assist the new local government since they assumed there would retribution if Turkish forces returned. Until the British could demonstrate to the local populace that the Turks would never return, recruitment of their service was difficult.

To prove that they weren't going to be leaving soon, the British progressed well beyond projects of military necessity. Lt. Col. Arthur Wilson, himself a Civil Commissioner, clearly defined his mission as a replacement of the Turkish administration, "to make good by successive installments the promises of liberty, justice, and prosperity so freely made to the Arab inhabitants at the very outset of the campaign."[168] Gertrude Bell, typified this dedication by commenting on February 8, 1918, "We are pledged here. It would be an unthinkable crime to abandon those who have loyally served us."[169]

An important step in the establishment of a viable civil administration was the painstaking collection, organization, and systematization of information. Reassigned to the Political Department, Gertrude Bell played a key role in classifying tribal and other data, beginning with information obtained from the Intelligence Department and updating it based upon the continued British advance. By February 1917, she could claim that her office had not only organized a mass of data, but all tribal, and some other material, was available in official circulars. They had compiled an exact accounting of the country as the British found it.[170]

Thus, Brownlow had to create an effective civil administration with neither the assistance of historical records nor the cooperation of the local population. The British inherited a Turkish administration, which consisted of several departments: Department of Pious Foundations (Waqf), Land Records (Tapu), Crown Lands, Customs, Ottoman Public Debt, Excise, and Tobacco Regie. With the exception of Customs,

Brownlow assumed control of these redundant and inherently inefficient departments, and he also took control of educational institutions and municipal finances.[171] While he combined some departments of the former Turkish administration and temporarily eliminated the Tobacco Regie, the overall structure remained,[172] and only the ex-official members of the local population whom the British considered honest, remained employed. Most records in each department remained in Turkish, although receipts and all other official business were changed to Arabic, an adjustment that the local population welcomed.[173]

The British also fostered the development of a press with, on November 29, 1914, the establishment of The Basra Times, which was a government paper until commercialization in 1921. Later, The Baghdad Times published in English and Arabic, becoming an Arab government press in 1921.

The British also changed the primary currency from the Turkish Lira to the Indian Rupee, and established the exchange rate by proclamation, which didn't sit well with the local population. A viable currency system became a necessity in the light of developing revenues from taxation and customs duties, so the British set up branches of the Imperial Bank of Persia which dealt in rupees, rather than gold as in Arabia; however, they still faced the challenge of limited acceptance of paper notes, especially in Baghdad. Constant assessment and timely response precluded a currency crisis, and the government passed a rigorous audit. The British even implemented an interim postage stamp system.[175]

Eventually, even the military learned that "fining" was a

more effective retaliation and deterrent against Arab marauders than burning and shelling villages.[180]

The civil administration also arranged for the billeting of British troops in local residences. While the British paid fair rent for all local housing that billeted their soldiers, they forced the local inhabitants to vacate these buildings. Not surprisingly, this requirement caused friction and ultimately became one of the principal grievances of the local population against the British occupation.[176]

After the first four months of occupation, the local population in Basra responded positively to the British even though the Turkish military was still close by. Trade recommenced and the bazaars were busy, and most importantly, the British had managed to restore law and order. Overall, British successes in its early civil administration in Iraq were facilitated by Britain's long-standing commercial activities in the vilayet. Subsequent victories in Qurna in late 1914 and Amara, Nasiriya, and Kut-al-Amara in 1915 required the British to expand their civil administration, with deputy military commissioners established in each of these newly occupied cities along with assistant political officers.[177]

However, in general, there remained a tension between the Civil Administration and the Army throughout operations in Mesopotamia. First, running the civil service was a major drain of military manpower. The Civil Administration drew heavily on personnel from India: the Indian Army, the Reserve of Officers, Civil Service, Imperial and Provincial Police Forces, as well as those who had been serving in the Sudan, Egypt, and England.

Townshend commented in late 1915 that he asked in vain for the return of his British soldiers to 6th Indian Division who were functioning as policemen, clerks, and sundry augmenters to help run and protect the river transport.[178] The other major tension resulted from differing attitudes about the Arabs between the newer civil administrators who entered a subdued Iraq and those who remembered only Arab hostility, theft, and rapacity.[179]

The fall of Baghdad in 1917 ushered in a new phase in the British occupation of Iraq. Despite his protests, the British government ordered General Maude, General Officer Commanding of Iraq, to proclaim: "our Armies have not come into your Cities and Lands as Conquerors, or enemies, but as Liberators. Therefore, I am commanded to invite you, through your Nobles and Elders and Representatives, to participate in the management of your civil affairs in collaboration with the Political Representatives of Great Britain... so that you may unite with your kinsmen in the North, East, South, and West."[181] This declaration further demonstrated the rift between the Foreign Office and the Viceroy on future policy in Iraq. The Foreign Office continued to promote an independent Arab kingdom, something that the Viceroy and Maude opposed.[182]

Based on the Sykes-Picot Agreement, the Asquith government assumed that Basra would eventually be ruled by a predominately British regime, and Baghdad would be a British protectorate led by an independent Arab government. Consequently, in May 1917, the British government ordered Maude to set up a primarily Arab government in Baghdad separate from Basra with British officials serving only as advisors.[183]

In Baghdad, as in Basra, the retreating Ottoman forces not only took what records they could and destroyed those they could not, but they also ransacked the bazaars and pilfered gold and goods from local businesses.[184] Similarly, the British found it very difficult to recruit local residents to assist the new civil administration: "Every Arab in Baghdad knew that those inhabitants of the country who had taken service with the British at Kut had been tortured and put to death." Until local residents were convinced that the Turks would never return, they feared cooperating with the British. Furthermore, unlike the residents in Basra who were mostly Shia and poorly treated by the Turks, the majority of the population in Baghdad were Sunni and enjoyed better overall treatment by the former Ottoman administration. Many of the locals who had served in the Turkish civil service still felt loyal to their former masters, and did not welcome the British as openly as Shia dominated Basra.[186]

Maude did not delegate the affairs of the civil administration to the military governor nor his chief political officer. In accordance with direction from the Lloyd George government, he initially put the city under martial law and formed a minimal civil administration until a definitive policy on Baghdad's future could be decided.[187] Furthermore, he "did most of the General Staff work himself" and tasked his principal staff officers to organize the civil administration.[188]

Maude appointed General C. J. Hawker as the Military Governor of Baghdad and attempted to micromanage his work as well as many facets of the civil administration. He and Sir

Percy Cox also disagreed on the policy toward local Arabs, with Cox wanting to extend British influence to the countryside surrounding Baghdad and Maude not wanting to disperse troops far outside the city because of an expected Turkish counterattack.[189] Cox's job, thus, became increasingly difficult because of Maude's command style and their differences in policy.[190] In fact, Cox could not even communicate with the War Cabinet without coordinating his telegrams with Maude first.[191]

To solve the impasse between Maude and Cox, the Lloyd George government, in consultation with General Robertson, decided to make Cox "Civil Commissioner" in July 1917, and authorized him to send reports on the political and economic situation directly to the War Cabinet. However, "Maude would still have the higher authority, and the reports would still pass through his hands." This change in designation signaled the Lloyd George government and the Viceroy's support of Cox, but Maude still had the final overall authority. However, this conflict became moot after Maude died in November 1917, and Maude's replacement, General Marshall, and Cox cooperated more harmoniously.[192]

From 1917 to 1920, the British tried to billet as many soldiers and government civilians in Baghdad as possible, for both climatic reasons and administrative convenience. Over 190 houses on the Tigris, once occupied by local notables, were occupied, and although the British paid rent at the prewar rate plus 10 percent, the scale on which these houses were occupied caused resentment by local residents. Furthermore, cordon searches, the enforcement of sanitary measures, and the frequent issuance of regulations, often viewed as arbitrary by the local populace, were also sources of frustration. Clearly, Maude and his principal staff officers made no observable attempt in Baghdad to apply the experiences learned by Brownlow in Basra. Despite the irritation caused by some of the British policies, most residents in Baghdad tolerated their new occupiers but were slow to trust them.[193]

Since, at that time, the British assumed that the French would eventually take over the Mosul vilayet in accordance with the Sykes-Picot Agreement, they only expected to set up a temporary military administration. Marshall appointed Lieutenant Colonel Leachman as the military governor of Mosul and the political officer in charge of the Mosul vilayet.[194]

British forces had an easier time of creating a civil administration in Mosul than they did in Basra or Baghdad, since the formal end of hostilities between Turkey and Britain prompted the former Ottoman authorities to leave most of the historical civil administration records intact. Additionally, since the fate of Mosul would not be formally decided until 1923, and many Turks wanted Mosul to remain under Turkish control, many former Ottoman officials stayed in Mosul after British forces arrived rather than evacuating the city.[195]

Some Ottoman officers, even after the Empire had signed an Armistice with the British, were still selling military supplies, burning civil records, and even recruiting irregulars to resist British influence in the vilayet. Leachman quickly ensured law and order in Mosul by raiding the houses of former Turkish officials, enforcing a nightly curfew with deadly force, including the shooting of a few looters. He also appointed local notables to official well-paid positions, ordering them to provide a local police force until a permanent force could be established.[196]

Cox departed Iraq in early 1918 and Wilson, his deputy, assumed control of the civil administration, working as acting civil commissioner from 1918-20. Because of the lack of a coherent policy from the Lloyd George government, Wilson initiated a direct type of rule and drew from his colonial experiences to formulate the civil administration. Consequently, he attempted to rule Iraq "modeled largely on Britain's imperial structure in India."[197]

Wilson abolished elected municipal councils established by the Ottomans and installed political officers in sixteen administrative districts, with assistant political officers serving in major cities. In 1917, only fifty-nine British officers served in the civil administration, but by 1920 there were 1,022. By contrast, Iraqis occupied fewer than 4 percent of the senior governmental positions in 1920.[198]

Wilson organized the overall civil administration into seven departments, two of which (education and police) he controlled directly: revenue, finance, judicial, public works, health department, education, and police. The revenue department consisted of the special taxes, irrigation, agriculture, survey, and land registration sub-departments, while the finance department was made up of customs, government presses, and enemy trading sub-departments. The judicial system administered the Iraqi Code for city dwellers, while the Tribal Criminal and Civil Disputes Regulations (TCCDR) applied to tribal or rural subjects. The railroad and telegraph sub-departments made up the public works department while the health department consisted of the medical and quarantine sub-department, as well as the weather bureau. His governing policies and the structure of his civil administration demonstrated that, in contrast to Britain's wartime declarations, little self-determination existed in Iraq after World War I.

Of particular interest is the re-organization of the health and educational systems.

The British inherited a dysfunctional education system in Iraq. Although the Ottoman educational system appeared well organized on paper, the British found it poorly administered in practice. Overall, the intent of the Turkish educational system was to "Ottomanize the Arabs."[199] Although most Iraqi children could speak and write Turkish, their Arabic grammar was poor; their knowledge of history, geography and arithmetic was inadequate; and they had almost no knowledge of mathematics, science, the antiquities, literature or art.[200]

The British reorganized the educational system by focusing on primary schools first. Major H.E. Bowman, head of the educational department in Iraq and former head of the same department in the British administration of Egypt, concentrated on appointing and training qualified teachers. The war had removed most of the teachers of the old system and there were not enough trained teachers to staff the remaining primary schools. Unfortunately, these reforms were impeded after the capture of Baghdad because the primary schools there "were nearly all looted by the mob."[201] Along with finding qualified teachers, Bowman revamped the curriculum to include instruction in the Arabic language for most schools and Turkish, Persian, and Kurdish in regions where those languages were spoken. Some schools also taught English, but only as a second language.

Bowman also promoted religious instruction dependent on the student's preference or family faith, in contrast to the old Turkish administration where only Sunni Islam was taught. He organized troops of Boy Scouts and promoted education for females, something practically nonexistent under the Turks. He also did away with the old uniform code that required male students to wear European-style clothes and a fez. He encouraged Arab-style dress and did not allow schools to fly the British flag or its students to swear allegiance to Britain or any other nation.[202]

The British eventually developed secondary schools as well, although parochial and denominational schools were the main providers of this level of education, and they intended to establish secondary education in larger towns, primarily to provide an eventual path to government service.[203] In reference to maktabs or Islamic religious schools, the British continued to support their existence, despite their contemptuous view of their educational value, normally through Waqf funds left over from the Ottoman administration.[204] In 1924, Dobbs stated, "[the muktabs] keep alive the mullas [sic] at the expense of the eyesight, health, and intelligence of their pupils."[257] This policy of support for the Islamic schools is consistent with the British tolerance of all other religious schools that operated in Iraq (e.g.,

Catholic, Protestant, Jewish, etc.). Bowman also continued supporting commercial and technical schools and managed to open both a training college for teachers and a law school in Baghdad by 1920. Overall, despite the lack of resources, the British attempted to provide an efficient and well-rounded educational system that tried to accommodate all ethnicities and religions.

Sati al-Husri, Feisal's Director-General of Education from 1923-7, subsequently used this educational foundation to "establish a coherent and controlled national ideology throughout the school system." Al-Husri, a Syrian ideologue, promoted pan-Arabism throughout the educational system in an attempt to unify the disparate ethnicities and religions of the Iraqi population. During his tenure, the curriculum of each school celebrated Iraq's proud history and made "analogies to Iraq as the Arab Piedmont or Prussia."[206] This nationalism was inherently anti-British and its proponents continually challenged the monarchy until its end in 1958.

The British also had to revitalize the Iraqi health system.

A major from the Indian Medical Service began a civil medical system on December 30, 1914, becoming the first Civil Surgeon. The Port Health and Quarantine Services, a civil service which helped the Army, dealt with plague in the winter of 1916 and the spring of 1917, and the 1918 influenza outbreak, which did not hit Mesopotamia as hard as it did Persia and Europe.[174] Arthur Lawley, a Red Cross Commissioner, visited Basra and Amara in early 1916, and noted that Basra had an adequate water supply, an effective "anti-fly" crusade, and sound sanitation. The inhabitants had to conform to these regulations and benefited from them.

Although the Turkish system allowed for a twenty-bed hospital in each major city plus a few outpatient (dispensary) doctors and pharmacists, the war had completely disrupted the Ottoman health service. When the British entered Baghdad in 1917, they only found "a few medical officers and some French nuns who nursed the sick in the Baghdad hospital."[263] To best protect friendly forces and provide for the local population, the British quickly set out to rebuild the infrastructure of the Iraqi health system.

By the end of 1920, the British had built a health system staffed by more than 1,000 personnel: 10 percent British, 14 percent Indian, and 76 percent Iraqi. Twenty-eight hospitals and fifty-one dispensaries were operating full time and municipal health departments were located in Basra, Baghdad, and Mosul. Specialist institutions (e.g., Ophthalmic, Pathological, etc.) operated in Baghdad and Basra, and to stem the spread of disease, a quarantine station at Khanaqin. Overall, between 1921-1926, Iraqi hospitals and dispensaries admitted 100,813 total inpatients and 6,151,852 total outpatients respectively.[208]

Despite these successes in health and education, the rebellion against British rule in 1920 and the realities of declining budgets motivated the British to quickly find a means of reducing its investment in Iraq in terms of manpower and material resources. However, the British still wanted its influence to endure in Iraq because of the economic and strategic opportunities. Therefore, from 1920-6, the British had to devise a means of maintaining law and order in the country without substantial military forces.

In October 1920, the military occupation formally ended and Cox returned to assume the role of High Commissioner, at which he served until 1923. Sir Henry Dobbs replaced Cox and served as High Commissioner until 1929.

In order to satisfy its obligations under the League of Nations Mandate, the British began turning over all-governmental institutions to tribal sheikhs and lower governmental authorities. To achieve this goal, Cox restored administrative districts and municipal councils that existed under the Ottomans, and although, all Iraqi governmental institutions had British advisors, Iraqis began to replace British political officers in the administrative districts (except in southern Kurdistan). As a consequence, from 1920 to 1923 the number of British and Indian officers significantly decreased, from 2,035 to 1,270, with British government officers dropping from 364 to 181.[210]

The investment in power to the tribal sheiks was inherently problematic since it was in contrast to the actions taken by the Turks and significantly altered the social structure of Iraqi society. During their occupation of Iraq, the Turks purposely empowered individual tribesmen and tribal sub-groups to weaken the prestige and legitimacy of existing tribal leaders, thus leaving the sheikh with a nebulous relationship towards his fellow tribesmen. This policy of "divide-and-rule" prompted internal and external tribal rivalries that worked to the advantage of the Ottoman administration.[211]

In return for obedience and the maintenance of law and order in their tribal areas, sheikhs were initially given a monthly salary along with the some authority to regulate commercial traffic in their sectors. Ultimately, the sheikhs were authorized to manage land leases, agriculture production, and the collection of taxes from the lower levels of Iraqi society. As budgets declined, the British issued grants of land instead, and if an individual sheikh did not cooperate, he could be stripped of his authority and his tribe could lose land and formal recognition by British authorities.[213]

Unfortunately, despite the romantic view that the British held of Iraqi tribal sheikhs, they were just as susceptible to corruption as any other authoritative figure, and there was no mechanism in place to check any possible abuses committed against the lower levels of Iraqi society. Ultimately, this British policy impeded integration and weakened the development of Iraq's fragile national institutions.

During the military occupation, international convention required that the British maintain the existing laws in occupied territories, but the disappearance of the Turkish courts forced the British to make an adjustment. The British could not efficiently administer Turkish law (grounded in the Napoleonic Code)[214] so, when the British captured Basra, they had to create the Iraqi Occupied Territories Code (Iraqi Code), an ad-hoc justice system that was a combination of Indian and Turkish law. Courts convened in April 1915 and were conducted in Arabic. Because of the uncertainty of Baghdad's future when British forces arrived in 1917, Maude was not allowed to administer the Iraqi

Code and the looting had made the immediate opening of civil courts impossible. Consequently, the British imposed martial law in Baghdad until the end of 1917. During this period, military or political officers oversaw all criminal cases involving the local populace.[215]

The British intended to continue the administration of Turkish law in Baghdad, but practicality prompted another adjustment. In 1918, the British introduced elements of the Egyptian code (also grounded in the Napoleonic Code) into the existing Turkish law to best fit the conditions in Baghdad. This new ad-hoc civil law was later applied to Basra and Mosul in 1919 as well[216] and it endured until the end of the monarchy in 1958. These new courts tried capital crimes and virtually all other penal (criminal) and civil (monetary) cases except crimes against British forces, and only the General Officer Commanding of British forces in Iraq, in coordination with the chief political officer, had the authority to order the death penalty.[217] The British also improved the efficiency and integrity of the administration of this law by reducing the number of courts, carefully screening judges, and raising judge's salaries.[218]

By 1919, Courts of First Instance were set up in Baghdad, Hillah, Baquba, Basra, and Mosul. Three judges oversaw each court; a British judge served as the President of the court, accompanied by two Iraqi judges. In penal cases, Courts of First Instance were made up of four classes of courts: 1) Courts of Session that held unlimited jurisdiction; 2) Magistrates of the First Class (political officers and British judges) that could pass sentences of imprisonment not exceeding two years; 3)

Magistrates of the Second Class (assistant political officers) that could pass sentences of imprisonment not exceeding six months; and 4) Magistrates of the Third Class (anyone appointed by the civil or high commissioner) that could pass sentences of imprisonment not exceeding one month. In civil cases, Courts of First Instance held unlimited jurisdiction but Small Cause (Small Claims) courts, commonly known as Peace Courts, handled cases involving lower levels of monetary liability. The Court of Appeal in Baghdad served as the final court of appeal for both penal and civil cases. A British judge, also accompanied by two Iraqi judges, oversaw this court as well.[219]

Iraqis living in rural or tribal areas were subject to another code articulated in the TCCDR. This code endured with few changes until the end of the Mandate in 1932. It was first drawn up in 1916 by Sir Henry Dobbs, who had worked as Revenue and Judicial Commissioner in Baluchistan from 1909-11, sanctioned by British forces in 1918, and formalized by royal decree in 1924. The British enacted the TCCDR partly due to their view that the tribal sheikh ruled in a vertical structure, was democratically elected by his fellow tribe members, and was unspoiled by modernity (with all of its associated complexities and corruptions) unlike his city dwelling counterparts.[220] This code originated from the policy of British Colonel Robert Sandeman, who served as the Deputy Commissioner of the Dara Ghazi Khan district in Baluchistan in the northwestern frontier of India in the nineteenth century. His model of "humane imperialism" recognized the dominion of tribal sheikhs and ruled through them.[221] Despite the fact the TCCDR had been formulated to apply to one specific population with its own unique ethnic, social, and economic characteristics, the British applied it, with no discernable modification, to the Iraqis as well. Thus, "the Baluchistan and Iraqi tribes were conceptually homogenized into one undifferentiated group."[222]

The TCCDR enabled the local political officer to refer cases to "a majlis, or tribal court, consisting of sheikhs or arbiters selected according to tribal usage. Unless the findings of this body were manifestly unjust or at variance with the facts of the case, the Political Officer would pass judgment in general accordance with it."[223] This overall system of justice was based on tribal custom, collective responsibility, and punishment.[224] Capital punishment was not used in settling tribal related disputes for fear of fueling blood feuds. Instead, if a member of a tribe committed murder against a member of another tribe, the guilty member's tribe, not the individual member who committed the crime, would be required to pay a fine (blood money).

The British also allowed Islamic (Sharia Law) courts existing under the Turkish administration to remain. These courts settled marriage, divorce, family relations, and inheritance (successions) matters, and a Court of Revision (Mejlis Tamyiz) was set up in Baghdad to handle appeals from these Islamic courts.[225] Proceedings in these Islamic courts also took place in the Arabic language.

Therefore, the British administered two separate systems of justice for the Iraqis, and which applied to each Iraqi was dependent upon on his social class and where he lived. The political officer for each administrative district (and later local Iraqi government officials) decided which system applied to each individual Iraqi.

Regarding oil, before World War I, the Ottoman government had authorized the Turkish Petroleum Company (TPC), an oil consortium, to prospect for oil in Iraq, but after the war, Germany and Turkey had to forfeit their shares in TPC to British, Dutch, French, and American oil companies. Although Iraq was promised a 20 percent allocation of oil revenues in 1920, the Iraqi government relinquished its share in exchange for enhanced royalty payments and the construction of a refinery and pipeline.[227] This agreement permitted the TPC authority to explore, produce, and market oil in Iraq for seventy-five years.[228] The Iraqis made this exchange in 1925 after Britain suggested that it might make substantial concessions to Turkey over the Mosul vilayet if Iraq did not give up its 20 percent claim. Under the terms of the concession, TPC remained a British-registered company and had all rights to exploration in all of Iraq, excluding Basra. In addition, the TPC had to select a fixed number of plots and begin drilling within a few years afterwards, paying the Iraqi government a mutually agreed upon sum for each metric ton of oil drilled.[229] In 1938, the exploration and drilling rights to the Basra vilayet were leased to the Basrah Petroleum Company (BPC), a TPC (renamed the Iraqi Petroleum Company in 1929) affiliate.[230] So, thanks to British governmental and commercial maneuvering, Iraq did not have control of or the ability to fully benefit from its potentially lucrative petroleum assets for many years.

Summing up, the British arrived in Iraq ill prepared to conduct both military and civil affairs beyond the Basra vilayet. Despite their overall lack of preparation, however, they did have successes, including: rapidly establishing law and order, maximizing existing governmental infrastructure, tolerating some of the local customs, facilitating economic activity, speaking the local language, and improving the quality of life by revitalizing the education and health systems.

On the negative side, the lack of consistent direction from London and India continually frustrated the attempts of British military commanders and political officers to execute a coherent policy in Iraq. This, when coupled with the British domination of Iraqi oil exploration and production, and Britain's failure to deliver on its frequent promises of liberty, limited economic expansion and slowed national development as well.

However, the most damaging policy affecting the civil administration of the country was the wholesale application of a tribal code originally meant for tribes in the northwestern frontier of India to the rural population in Iraq. This policy effectively prevented the separation of the executive and judicial branches of government, which, with the empowerment of the sheikhs, subjected the lower classes to the potential tyranny of midlevel officials. Overall, Britain's land policy and administration of justice impeded the integration of the Iraqi polity because it failed to provide a direct link from the central government to the individual Iraqi and thus prevented the people from identifying with the central government. Although the British promised liberty and a benevolent civil administration to all Iraqis, it ended up only privileging a select minority and oppressing the majority by proxy.

# CHAPTER 12

# ADVICE FROM LAWRENCE OF ARABIA

T.E. Lawrence, the famous Lawrence of Arabia, wrote this piece for The Arab Bulletin in August 1917 to provide suggestions to his fellow advisors who worked with the Arabs in Arabia. Lawrence offered specific suggestions based on his personal experience reinforced by insights from his academic background and years of experience in the region. A detailed account of his experiences during the Arab Revolt appeared in *Seven Pillars of Wisdom: A Triumph.* His thoughts and insights remain useful today.

Article From: THE ARAB BULLETIN
August 20, 1917

TWENTY-SEVEN ARTICLES
T.E. Lawrence

The following notes have been expressed in commandment form for greater clarity and to save words. They are, however, only my personal conclusions, arrived at gradually while I worked in the Hejaz and now put on paper as stalking horses for beginners in the Arab armies. They are meant to apply only to Bedu [Bedouin]; townspeople or Syrians require totally different treatment. They are of course not suitable to any other person's need, or applicable unchanged in any particular situation. Handling Hejaz Arabs is an art, not a science, with exceptions and no obvious rules. At the same time we have a great chance there; the Sherif [Feisel] trusts us, and has given us the position (towards his Government) which the Germans wanted to win in Turkey. If we are tactful, we can at once retain his goodwill and carry out our job, but to succeed we have got to put into it all the interest and skill we possess.

1. Go easy for the first few weeks. A bad start is difficult to atone for, and the Arabs form their judgments on externals that we ignore. When you have reached the inner circle in a tribe, you can do as you please with yourself and them.

2. Learn all you can about your Ashraf [tribal name] and Bedu. Get to know their families, clans and tribes, friends and enemies, wells, hills and roads. Do all this by listening and by indirect inquiry. Do not ask questions. Get to speak their dialect of Arabic, not yours. Until you can understand their allusions, avoid getting deep into conversation or you will drop bricks. Be a little stiff at first.

3. In matters of business deal only with the commander of the army, column, or party in which you serve. Never give orders to anyone at all, and reserve your directions or advice for the C.O., however great the temptation (for efficiency's sake) of dealing with his underlings. Your place is advisory, and your advice is due to the commander alone. Let him see that this is your conception of your duty, and that his is to be the sole executive of your joint plans.

4. Win and keep the confidence of your leader. Strengthen his prestige at your expense before others when you can. Never refuse or quash schemes he may put forward; but ensure that they are put forward in the first instance privately to you. Always approve them, and after praise modify them insensibly, causing the suggestions to come from him, until they are in accord with your own opinion. When you attain this point, hold him to it, keep a tight grip of his ideas, and push them forward as firmly as possibly, but secretly, so that to one but himself (and he not too clearly) is aware of your pressure.

5. Remain in touch with your leader as constantly and unobtrusively as you can. Live with him, that at meal times and at audiences you may be naturally with him in his tent. Formal visits to give advice are not so good as the constant dropping of ideas in casual talk. When stranger sheikhs come in for the first time to swear allegiance and offer service, clear out of the tent. If their first impression is of foreigners in the confidence of the Sherif, it will do the Arab cause much harm.

6. Be shy of too close relations with the subordinates of the expedition. Continual intercourse with them will make it impossible for you to avoid going behind or beyond the instructions that the Arab C.O. has given them on your advice, and in so disclosing the weakness of his position you altogether destroy your own.

7. Treat the sub-chiefs of your force quite easily and lightly. In this way you hold yourself above their level. Treat the leader, if a Sherif [local leader descended from Mohammed], with respect. He will return your manner and you and he will

then be alike, and above the rest. Precedence is a serious matter among the Arabs, and you must attain it.

8. Your ideal position is when you are present and not noticed. Do not be too intimate, too prominent, or too earnest. Avoid being identified too long or too often with any tribal sheikh, even if C.O. of the expedition. To do your work you must be above jealousies, and you lose prestige if you are associated with a tribe or clan, and its inevitable feuds. Sherifs are above all blood-feuds and local rivalries, and form the only principle of unity among the Arabs. Let your name therefore be coupled always with a Sherif's, and share his attitude towards the tribes. When the moment comes for action put yourself publicly under his orders. The Bedu will then follow suit.

9. Magnify and develop the growing conception of the Sherifs as the natural aristocracy of the Arabs. Intertribal jealousies make it impossible for any sheikh to attain a commanding position, and the only hope of union in nomad Arabs is that the Ashraf be universally acknowledged as the ruling class. Sherifs are half-townsmen, half-nomad, in manner and life, and have the instinct of command. Mere merit and money would be insufficient to obtain such recognition; but the Arab reverence for pedigree and the Prophet gives hope for the ultimate success of the Ashraf.

10. Call your Sherif 'Sidi' in public and in private. Call other people by their ordinary names, without title. In intimate conversation call a Sheikh 'Abu Annad', 'Akhu Alia' or some similar by-name.

11. The foreigner and Christian is not a popular person in

Arabia. However friendly and informal the treatment of yourself may be, remember always that your foundations are very sandy ones. Wave a Sherif in front of you like a banner and hide your own mind and person. If you succeed, you will have hundreds of miles of country and thousands of men under your orders, and for this it is worth bartering the outward show.

12. Cling tight to your sense of humor. You will need it every day. A dry irony is the most useful type, and repartee of a personal and not too broad character will double your influence with the chiefs. Reproof, if wrapped up in some smiling form, will carry further and last longer than the most violent speech. The power of mimicry or parody is valuable, but use it sparingly, for wit is more dignified than humour. Do not cause a laugh at a Sherif except among Sherifs.

13. Never lay hands on an Arab; you degrade yourself. You may think the resultant obvious increase of outward respect a gain to you, but what you have really done is to build a wall between you and their inner selves. It is difficult to keep quiet when everything is being done wrong, but the less you lose your temper the greater your advantage. Also then you will not go mad yourself.

14. While very difficult to drive, the Bedu are easy to lead, if: have the patience to bear with them. The less apparent your interferences the more your influence. They are willing to follow your advice and do what you wish, but they do not mean you or anyone else to be aware of that. It is only after the end of all annoyances that you find at bottom their real fund of goodwill.

15. Do not try to do too much with your own hands. Better

the Arabs do it tolerably than that you do it perfectly. It is their war, and you are to help them, not to win it for them. Actually, also, under the very odd conditions of Arabia, your practical work will not be as good as, perhaps, you think it is.

16. If you can, without being too lavish, forestall presents to yourself. A well-placed gift is often most effective in winning over a suspicious sheikh. Never receive a present without giving a liberal return, but you may delay this return (while letting its ultimate certainty be known) if you require a particular service from the giver. Do not let them ask you for things, since their greed will then make them look upon you only as a cow to milk.

17. Wear an Arab headcloth when with a tribe. Bedu have a malignant prejudice against the hat, and believe that our persistence in wearing it (due probably to British obstinacy of dictation) is founded on some immoral or irreligious principle. A thick headcloth forms a good protection against the sun, and if you wear a hat your best Arab friends will be ashamed of you in public.

18. Disguise is not advisable. Except in special areas, let it be clearly known that you are a British officer and a Christian. At the same time, if you can wear Arab kit when with the tribes, you will acquire their trust and intimacy to a degree impossible in uniform. It is, however, dangerous and difficult. They make no special allowances for you when you dress like them. Breaches of etiquette not charged against a foreigner are not condoned to you in Arab clothes. You will be like an actor in a foreign theatre, playing a part day and night for months, without rest, and for an anxious stake. Complete success, which is when the Arabs forget

your strangeness and speak naturally before you, counting you as one of themselves, is perhaps only attainable in character: while half-success (all that most of us will strive for; the other costs too much) is easier to win in British things, and you yourself will last longer, physically and mentally, in the comfort that they mean. Also then the Turks will not hang you, when you are caught.

19. If you wear Arab things, wear the best. Clothes are significant among the tribes, and you must wear the appropriate, and appear at ease in them. Dress like a Sherif, if they agree to it.

20. If you wear Arab things at all, go the whole way. Leave your English friends and customs on the coast, and fall back on Arab habits entirely. It is possible, starting thus level with them, for the European to beat the Arabs at their own game, for we have stronger motives for our action, and put more heart into it than they. If you can surpass them, you have taken an immense stride toward complete success, but the strain of living and thinking in a foreign and half-understood language, the savage food, strange clothes, and stranger ways, with the complete loss of privacy and quiet, and the impossibility of ever relaxing your watchful imitation of the others for months on end, provide such an added stress to the ordinary difficulties of dealing with the Bedu, the climate, and the Turks, that this road should not be chosen without serious thought.

21. Religious discussions will be frequent. Say what you like about your own side, and avoid criticism of theirs, unless you know that the point is external, when you may score heavily

by proving it so. With the Bedu, Islam is so all-pervading an element that there is little religiosity, little fervor, and no regard for externals. Do not think from their conduct that they are careless. Their conviction of the truth of their faith, and its share in every act and thought and principle of their daily life is so intimate and intense as to be unconscious, unless roused by opposition. Their religion is as much a part of nature to them as is sleep or food.

22. Do not try to trade on what you know of fighting. The Hejaz confounds ordinary tactics. Learn the Bedu principles of war as thoroughly and as quickly as you can, for till you know them your advice will be no good to the Sherif. Unnumbered generations of tribal raids have taught them more about some parts of the business than we will ever know. In familiar conditions they fight well, but strange events cause panic. Keep your unit small. Their raiding parties are usually from one hundred to two hundred men, and if you take a crowd they only get confused. Also their sheikhs, while admirable company commanders, are too 'set' to learn to handle the equivalents of battalions or regiments. Don't attempt unusual things, unless they appeal to the sporting instinct Bedu have so strongly, unless success is obvious. If the objective is a good one (booty) they will attack like fiends, they are splendid scouts, their mobility gives you the advantage that will win this local war, they make proper use of their knowledge of the country (don't take tribesmen to places they do not know), and the gazelle-hunters, who form a proportion of the better men, are great shots at visible targets. A sheikh from one tribe cannot give orders to

men from another; a Sherif is necessary to command a mixed tribal force. If there is plunder in prospect, and the odds are at all equal, you will win. Do not waste Bedu attacking trenches (they will not stand casualties) or in trying to defend a position, for they cannot sit still without slacking. The more unorthodox and Arab your proceedings, the more likely you are to have the Turks cold, for they lack initiative and expect you to. Don't play for safety.

23. The open reason that Bedu give you for action or inaction may be true, but always there will be better reasons left for you to divine. You must find these inner reasons (they will be denied, but are none the less in operation) before shaping your arguments for one course or other. Allusion is more effective than logical exposition: they dislike concise expression. Their minds work just as ours do, but on different premises. There is nothing unreasonable, incomprehensible, or inscrutable in the Arab. Experience of them, and knowledge of their prejudices will enable you to foresee their attitude and possible course of action in nearly every case.

24. Do not mix Bedu and Syrians, or trained men and tribesmen. You will get work out of neither, for they hate each other. I have never seen a successful combined operation, but many failures. In particular, ex-officers of the Turkish army, however Arab in feelings and blood and language, are hopeless with Bedu. They are narrow minded in tactics, unable to adjust themselves to irregular warfare, clumsy in Arab etiquette, swollen- headed to the extent of being incapable of politeness to a tribesman for more than a few minutes, impatient, and, usually,

helpless without their troops on the road and in action. Your orders (if you were unwise enough to give any) would be more readily obeyed by Beduins than those of any Mohammedan Syrian officer. Arab townsmen and Arab tribesmen regard each other mutually as poor relations, and poor relations are much more objectionable than poor strangers.

25. In spite of ordinary Arab example, avoid too free talk about women. It is as difficult a subject as religion, and their standards are so unlike our own that a remark, harmless in English, may appear as unrestrained to them, as some of their statements would look to us, if translated literally.

26. Be as careful of your servants as of yourself. If you want a sophisticated one you will probably have to take an Egyptian, or a Sudani, and unless you are very lucky he will undo on trek much of the good you so laboriously effect. Arabs will cook rice and make coffee for you, and leave you if required to do unmanly work like cleaning boots or washing. They are only really possible if you are in Arab kit. A slave brought up in the Hejaz is the best servant, but there are rules against British subjects owning them, so they have to be lent to you. In any case, take with you an Ageyli [tribal name] or two when you go up country. They are the most efficient couriers in Arabia, and understand camels.

27. The beginning and ending of the secret of handling Arabs is unremitting study of them. Keep always on your guard; never say an unnecessary thing: watch yourself and your companions all the time: hear all that passes, search out what is going on beneath the surface, read their characters, discover their

tastes and their weaknesses and keep everything you find out to yourself. Bury yourself in Arab circles, have no interests and no ideas except the work in hand, so that your brain is saturated with one thing only, and you realize your part deeply enough to avoid the little slips that would counteract the painful work of weeks. Your success will be proportioned to the amount of mental effort you devote to it.

# CHAPTER 13

# IN THE NEWS

Article From: CURRENT OPINION
May, 1922

THE RISING POWER OF ISLAM

FOLLOWING the Great War has come something almost as great, tho few realize it. That thing is what Lothrop Stoddard calls "the new world of Islam." Mr. Stoddard has written a book on the subject, which is attracting international attention. It appears at a time when the Near East Conference of Allied Foreign Ministers in Paris has virtually rewritten the Treaty of Sèvres to the advantage of Turkey, and when riots in India and Egypt, guerilla warfare in northern Africa and outbreaks in Syria are all being traced to Mohammedan influence. The recent appeal of the Government of India to London in behalf of Turkey was also, of course, inspired by Islam, and, taken together, these signs would seem to justify Mr. Stoddard's statement: "The entire world of Islam is to-day in profound ferment. From Morocco to China and from Turkestan to the Congo, the 250,000,000 followers of the Prophet Mohammed are stirring to new ideas, new impulses, new aspirations. A gigantic transformation is taking place whose results must affect all mankind."

Mr. Stoddard, in an earlier book, "The Rising Tide of

Color," tried to show that the ascendancy of the white race is threatened by the colored races. He is concerned, now, with the ascendancy of a religion that imposes on its devotees a governmental and social code. It may be that he is an alarmist when he speaks of a possible "crisis which within ten years will bring war between Christian Europe and Moslem nations," but his writings are quoted by President Harding and by Lord Northcliffe, and the latter, after a trip round the world, is at pains to make clear that Islam is a core of unrest in three of the five "trouble centers of the world" – Japan, China, India, Egypt, Palestine.

Mohammedanism is younger by 600 years than any of the great religions of the world. Its dawn was bright, and it flowered in a Saracenic civilization in which the ancient cultures of Greece, Rome and Persia were revitalized by Arab vigor. This period gave way to one in which the Turk introduced a hard, narrow, ferocious spirit into the center of Islam, and was followed by a Reformation which Mr. Stoddard likens to the Protestant Reformation. Abd-el-Wahab was the Martin Luther of this Reformation. His movement was crushed, but his spirit lived on and helped to inspire the Bab movement in Persia and that veiled but very powerful Senussi fraternity in the North of Africa, which has been called the spiritual heart of Islam to-day.

The new Islam — in India, Egypt, Persia, the former Ottoman Empire — is a strangely contradictory faith. It mingles autocracy with democracy, and oscillates between proposals to restore the ancient faith and to incorporate the latest results of Occidental civilization. It is still, however, a missionary religion, and it fully appreciates the post-office, the railroad and other modern methods of rapidly interchanging ideas. It is also, to an extent, which the average Christian hardly appreciates, unified. A Moslem can feel himself a "national" citizen of any Islamic country, and cherishes, a fraternal feeling for all who share his faith.

The victors in the Great War who imagined that they were solving the Moslem problem by driving the Turk out of Europe were only aggravating that problem, as Mr. Stoddard sees it. They failed to take into account the unity of Mohammedans. As a result, the Moslem world was rewelded and revitalized as it had not been in centuries, and the ears of every Mohammedan were opened to propaganda for the freeing of every Moslem country now in tutelage or bondage to a European power.

Bolshevism was quick to take advantage of the opportunity, and Lenin's emissaries were soon working among the Mohammedans. There were startling developments and many converts made in Turkey, Persia, India, Afghanistan and the farther Orient. It almost seemed, Mr. Stoddard says, as if the reckless shortsightedness of Entente policy was driving into Lenin's arms multitudes who, under other conditions, would have avoided him.

For most Mohammedans are nationalists, not internationalists; are religious, not irreligious; believe in private property, and look to the Sultan as to a Pope. When the noted Bolshevik leader Zinoviev spoke before the "Congress of Eastern Peoples" called by the Soviet Government at Baku in the autumn of 1920, he endeavored to eradicate the religious beliefs and national loyalties of his hearers by preaching the class-war.

Bolshevism was a nine-days' wonder to the Mohammedan world, but as yet no real merging of the two has taken place. There is still time, Mr. Stoddard says, to forestall both a Bolshevist peril and the possibility of a war between Christian and Moslem nations. He goes on: "I predict increasing ferment and unrest throughout all Islam; a continued awakening to self-consciousness; an increasing dislike for Western domination.

"The result must inevitably be the diminution of white control in Asia and Africa.

"The vital question is whether shaking off white control will come with or without a cataclysm. The cataclysm may come. It will come if England and France pursue a shortsighted policy and by repressive measures drive liberal Mohammedans into the ranks of the extremists.

"I hope to see the cataclysm avoided by the adoption of a policy of gradual diminution of white control."

Article From: MANCHESTER GUARDIAN
June 24, 1920

MESOPOTAMIA

This blessed word means 35 millions to the British taxpayer. That is the first point that comes out of Mr. Asquith's strongly reasoned criticism of Government's Mesopotamian policy. Mr. Asquith is always cautious and "conservative" to a fault in his calculations, and it is not likely that his estimate errs by exaggeration. The first inference to be drawn is that, be the Mesopotamian policy right or wrong, wise or foolish, legal or illegal, it is useless to talk about retrenchment, it is vain to sigh for any reduction of income tax or excess profits duty or any other financial burden as long as the policy of territorial expansion - for that is what it comes to - is kept up. We are expecting for a greater military expenditure in regions technically outside the British Empire than the whole cost of our army in pre-war days. What is the use of nibbling at little bits of civilian expenditure when tens of millions are thrown about in this fashion? At the back of it, we all know, is the oil of Mosul. In the forefront Mr. Lloyd George places the grim figure of Mustapha Kemal and our duty to the Arab peoples. Does anyone consult the Arabs? Do they want an Anglo-India Administration, or would they form a government of their own with some backing of expert advice from us? Agreed that, having driven out the Turks, we could not leave the county without some provision for order. Was it necessary for us to rush in with a regular westernized administration, with punitive expeditions and machine-guns all complete? Mr. Lloyd George tells us that the resources of the country will all be ultimately at the disposal of Arab State. Do we take the Arabs into our confidence and seek from the first to enable them to govern their own country, and if so why do we need all this machinery, all these forces, all these punitive expeditions, and 35 millions from the British taxpayer? We should not need these things if we were establishing a political system on the basis of popular consent.

Behind all this lies a political issue of the first magnitude. Mr. Asquith very properly said that if we are counting on the utilization of resources of the country for our own benefit that was in flagrant contradiction with the Covenant of the League of Nations, and he denied that we have any legal status except as mandatories of the League. To this Mr. Lloyd George replied with an absolute denial that mandates were given by the League. Mandates, in Mr. Lloyd George's view, are given by the Allies to one another. That may be, but such material concessions are absolutely without legal authority. Article 22 of the Covenant is explicit on the point. The tutelage of "peoples not yet able to stand by themselves" is to "form a sacred trust of civilisation." It is to be entrusted to advanced nations, and "should be exercised" by them as mandatories on behalf of "the League." This is a part of the Covenant which Mr. Lloyd George signed on behalf of this country, and it binds us as clearly as anything in the treaties binds Germany to take over German or Turkish territory only as mandatories of the League and on the conditions laid down in the Covenant for such mandates. Grant that the Allies might provisionally agree among themselves as to the territories in which they would keep order. It is clear that in proceeding to establish themselves or one another as mandatories they were presuming upon their power and taking to themselves functions, which only the League can lawfully exercise. The very term mandate was never heard in this connection except in reference to the League. That, then, is the legal position. Mr. Lloyd George and the Allied Governments are coolly assuming that the League must accept as mandatories whomsoever they choose to designate - that is, they are putting it in a derisory position. Mr. Lloyd George may talk of an Arab State - a nebulous possibility of the future. If the League of Nations - with all the powers - including Russia, as parties - is not responsible for the defense of this State, then we are responsible. We have, that is, to defend frontiers hundreds of miles from the sea, and we shall not be in a position to do so when any great power is resurrected on the other side of that frontier. There are limits to the responsibilities of Empire and to the burdens, which the taxpayer will bear.

Article From: THE LONDON TIMES
June 23, 1920

MESOPOTAMIA AND ANATOLIA

The Army Estimates come before the House of Commons to-day, and they will require an unusual amount of explanation. Whatever may be said about them, we hope a tribute will be paid to the skill of Sir Charleh Harris, the Accounting Officer, who is steadily improving the method of presentation of these Estimated, and is gradually making them more intelligible to the layman. A welcome change is that most of the expenditure on the forces in occupied territories is now grouped for purposes of explanation in one place. We can thus begin to form some idea, for example, of what the British taxpayer is being called upon to spend in Mesopotamia. Yet the Estimates do not show the full cost of the troops at present in Mesopotamia or Persia, and there are various items about which the ardent desire of Sir Charles Harris to conceal nothing has apparently been checked for political reasons. The true number of British and Indian troops in Mesopotamia and Persia to-day is somewhere about 90,000, excluding the Air Force, and not the 70,503 shown in the Estimates. The total military expenditure under all heads must therefore be not the £21,605,000 stated, but a considerably larger sum. Mr. Churchill has substantially increased the net strength of the garrison of Mesopotamia in the last two months. Why has he done so? No specific provision is made anywhere for the 9,000 men under General Malleson now stationed at Meshed, in

North-West Persia; nor for their numerous camels, their motor transport, and the costly details of their paraphernalia. On another point the House of Commons should demand information, if the rules permit. What is the Air Force in Mesopotamia costing, and what is its strength? No clue can be found in the Air Estimates, and it seems to us that in a debate, which is likely to raise on broad lines the whole question of the cost of Mesopotamia, some explicit details under this head should be furnished. Nothing, again, is provided for expenditure on the civil administration, and this item, which is assuredly very heavy, does not figure in any of the Budget Estimates. Then there is no provision for the various little punitive expeditions in which the Mesopotamia Army of Occupation is frequently engaged. In various other respects the Mesopotamia and Persian portion of the Estimates can be riddled through and through, and we must again express the belief that at the present moment the Government are spending the taxpayers' money in these two countries at the rate of £50,000,000 annually. A full account of their prospective policy in the Middle East should be furnished at once.

Letter to the Editor: THE LONDON TIMES
June 21, 1920

Sir, By constantly drawing attention to our adventure in Mesopotamia, and to our financial commitments in that dreary land, you are undoubtedly performing a service to the British taxpayers, and is to be hoped that in time he will be sufficiently educated on the subject to realize that it is from his pockets the money is being taken to pay for an army in order to protect a country against itself, for that is really what it means.

Eastern peoples as a rule detest efficiency and sanitation, and although the Arab welcomed us when we were beating the Turk, and incidentally paying for everything bought in the country at rates far in excess of any prices before heard of, I doubt if he wishes to be civilized in a hurry, and certainly he resents excessive control and taxation. If, therefore, the new system is not likely to be permanently acceptable to the Arab community, or requires an army of occupation for many year until the people have become civilized and accepted our form of administration, is the British taxpayer to bear the cost? A great many people will think that charity begins at home and boots would rather see the British taxpayer's money spent in this country.

If my surmises are correct, that not only are we attempting far too much in Mesopotamia, but also we are doing it with an inferior staff. The Civil Commissioner himself, although possessed of inexhaustible energy, is a political officer with no previous experience of administration, and what is required first and foremost in Mesopotamia is an administrator of the type of the first Lord Cromer. Such a man is, however, exceedingly difficult to procure in these days; indeed, too great have been our losses during the war, not only through casualties, but because the rising generation has been taken away from its legitimate studies for a period of five years.

It is, I submit, of little practical value at this stage to consider why we went to Mesopotamia, or why we remain there, because it is obvious that we cannot now evacuate the country, or even retire to the port of Basra and surrounding territory.

Our greatest expense is in the maintenance of the Army, and that could probably be reduced if we abandoned the idea of bringing the whole of Mesopotamia simultaneously under rigid control. It should be sufficient to have European officers and garrisons at the very few towns of importance, and we should, of course, have to guard and maintain the lines of communication by river and rail, but the remainder of Mesopotamia should be left to work out its own salvation by degrees and by its own people. In that case there would be no such incidents as the murder of British officers at Tel-Afar and consequent punitive expeditions; the tribes would confine their energies to killing each other as they have done for hundreds of years past, and they would be better and quieter if left alone. The administration under the mandate would lose a certain amount of revenue but would, gain by a reduction in military expenditure; whilst by degrees and all in good time civilization, as we know it, would spread throughout the country.

We should also, even in parts of the country directly under

our administration, go slowly, and refrain from forcing on the people town councils, improvement trusts, drainage and water supply, and all the other paraphernalia of civilization, more especially as the people themselves are unable to pay the bills; and lastly, we should exercise a rigid control over expenditure, especially on public works. Some works are essential but it must be borne in mind that whilst one engineer would insist on nothing short of absolute perfection whatever the cost, others are content to cut their coat according to their cloth, and many estimates for essential works which appear in the Budget with a lump sum allotment, and are passed without comment by the head of the administration, could be materially reduced by exercising economy.

In conclusion, I must repeat that I have never been a believer in the rapid development of Mesopotamia in any shape or form, but I do think that by a better form of administration, than obtains at present, we can make the mandate a success and greatly reduce the expenditure.

Article From: THE MORNING POST

TWO ADJOURNMENTS
June 16, 1920

Those concerned with British interests in the East have had once more to put up with a postponement of their expectations. Other engagements have prevented Lord Curzon from being able to make his promised statement on the situation in Mesopotamia and Persia, and Mr. Montagu has found reasons, which might have been guessed if he had not avowed them for deferring the debate on then Punjab riots. The time is overdue for the ventilation of both the subjects. In the absence of Parliamentary explanation, the question of our status in Mesopotamia has been brought to the front by the Shammar Arabs, who have captured and sacked the town of Tel Afar, only 40 miles from Mosul, burning the Government offices and killing the Government officials. The Political Officer in charge and three of those under him are reported to have fallen this affair, while two armored cars attempting to retrieve the situation fell into the hands of the Arabs. This is no isolated outbreak of disorder. The life, in fact, of a Political Officer who is sent to administer the tract north of Mosul is as precarious as that of a Cork constable. In six months we have lost six of these valuable officers, exclusive of the Tel Afar casualties. As soon as an officer is appointed to the post he is marked down by the tribal sharpshooters or assassins. His death involves an avenging expedition, which probably finds an empty village, sees no one, and loses some men as it returns. A recurrence of these incidents involves a heavy drain in money to add to the charge that the interesting country is already imposing on us.

The Public will expect Lord Curzon to say how the Government proposes to deal with the situation. The Kurdish frontier question promises to be a more formidable difficulty than the Indian frontier question, for one thing because of the geographical conditions, for another because the charge of guarding a frontier is very difficult thing for a population of 315 millions. It may be argued that the juice, or rather the oil, of Mesopotamia will be worth the trouble and cost of cracking the rind. The operation can be performed if we are prepared to get behind the Kurds; in other words, to make our frontier the Black Sea coast once for all. That, at any rate, would be an intelligent policy; and if Lord Curzon will only announce it the public will give it a fair consideration on the advice of the experts.

We were once said to have acquired India in a fit of absence of mind, and we seem to have drifted over Mesopotamia on currents of cross-purpose. The original expedition went to protect the Persian oilfields and Basra delta. Then General Townshend was ordered to advance on Baghdad to retrieve the prestige lost at Gallipoli. Next it was necessary to efface the effect of the fall of Kut. Baghdad gained, we were obliged to go on to secure the flank of Persia; and, finally, it is judged to be all important to retain Mosul, at the risk of rousing the suspicions of the French as well as the hostility of the Kurds, because of the richness of the oilfields. Oil is once more the magnet that draws us on. It may be that the prospect justifies the proceedings, but the British public, which only has the certainty of having to foot the bill, may claim to know how the chance stands. Equally as to the administration of Mesopotamia: is it to be under the Foreign Office, or the India Office, or the Government of India? At present it may be suspected of being carried on by a Ministry of Circumlocution. It is decided to form a separate Administration, which will assuredly come to pass sooner or later, it will be necessary to assert some sort of title for the Government. People may pay their taxes in the first instance by force of custom, but one cannot go on indefinitely taking this for granted. Suppose a Sheikh insists on the absolute property of his land and denies the right of Government to assess him for land revenue; will it be a satisfactory answer to say that the demand is made in virtue of a mandate conferred by a benevolent body called the Supreme Council or the League of Nations? But before all these questions may perhaps come, the primary one is why we are in Mesopotamia at all and why we should remain there. The usual answer is that it is very necessary to protect Persia. If it is asked what we are doing in Persia the reply comes that our position there is important for guarding of Mesopotamia. Finally, if the inquirer asks why we should trouble about either country we are told that the basis of the policy is the safe keeping of India, which, from another point of view, we seem anxious to part with altogether. There is certainly room for an authoritative statement, which would supply a coherent answer to all these perplexities.

Article From: THE LONDON TIMES
June 24, 1920

MR. LLOYD GEORGE
IN THE GARDEN OF EDEN.

In the House of Commons yesterday, in the debate on the Army Estimates, the Prime Minister made a long and rhetorical, but, for the most part, unpractical speech upon the question of Mesopotamia. Every one knows that Mesopotamia is the supposed location of the Garden of Eden. Mr. Lloyd George inverted the traditional story, and seemed to imagine himself as a tempting Adam whispering vague invitations to a particularly trustful Eve. Though he did not appear to realize it, he was really speaking to a roused and angry nation, indignant at the colossal waste of which his Government has been guilty, groaning beneath taxation, which need never have been imposed, and bewildered by the general decline, which is threatening the industries of the country. What answer had he to make to the unhappy taxpayers who are invited to pour millions upon millions into the arid wastes of Mesopotamia and the bare plains of Persia? Nothing at all. Mr. Asquith had confronted the Prime Minister with a cold, clear and studiously restrained indictment. Mr. Lloyd George evaded every count. He never attempted to reply to a single one of the searching points submitted to him. He sought refuge in windy generalities, which may have pleased his credulous supporters, but will not appease a nation whose business is developing creeping paralysis as a consequence of over-taxation and enormously wasteful expenditure. Mr. Asquith concluded his speech by asking whether the people of this country were to go on spending from £30,000,000 to £40,000,000 upon the region of Mesopotamia, which contains about two million inhabitants. Mr. Lloyd George made no direct answer, but left the public to understand by inference from his words that such is the intention. We can only say that he must have become completely oblivious of realities. Any British Government, however large its majority, which proposes to continue to force the British public to provide £40,000.000 a year for Mesopotamian semi-nomads will overtax the patience of the country.

Mr. Asquith's points were too numerous to cite in full, but we will take one or two of them by way of illustration. He asked about the force of 9,000 men under General Malleson in North-East Persia, and was told by Mr. Churchill that the numbers were "rather more" than half that figure. "We may confront Mr. Churchill with his own words. On the 8th instant he said in the House of Commons: " There is a force of some 9,000 Indian troops in East Persia." Where have half of them gone in the last few days? Mr. Churchill had himself admitted that it will take four or five months for these troops to evacuate the country. Mr. Asquith contended that there were more troops in Mesopotamia than were shown in the Estimates. He got an involved answer on that point, which showed that he was right. Mr. Asquith pointed out that the admitted cost of the troops was higher than the Estimates, and his charge was received in silence. He challenged the Government on an item of £1,667,000 for "works" and "railway construction" and £1,000,000 for land. The Prime Minister interjected the remark, "You will get the information," but in fact no information was given. Last night a majority of the House of Commons actually voted nearly £3,000,000 for works of which it was told nothing, for payment only of immense cantonments in a region the future of which has still to be decided, and for land the very location of which remained undisclosed. Such is the new passion for "economy" among Coalition members. Mr. Asquith further pointed out that there was token vote of £100 for civil administration, and asked where the money was being found for the purpose. Mr. Lloyd George audaciously replied that the civil administration was "paying its way" in Mesopotamia, a statement the venture brings to question. The civil and military administrations cannot be financially considered apart. How can any country be said to be "paying its way" when the British public are providing £40,000,000 a year for its protection?

Mr. Ornsby-Gore said that in 1918 -19 the sum raised in local taxation was £1,000,000, and that last year £5,000.000 was extracted from these two million pastoral and roving people by administrators eager to turn the Garden of Eden into a new paradise for Anglo-Indian officials. It was said, in the course of the debate, that the excessive taxation and the mutual hostility between the Arabs and the Indian troops were the real causes of the frequent outbreaks; and we believe the accusation to be true. Mr. Asquith demanded information about the Air Force in Mesopotamia, which does not figure in any of the Estimates. Mr. Lloyd George gave no answer. He was not concerned with facts; his business was delusive rhetoric. Later in the debate Sir Donald Maclean compelled Mr. Churchill to admit that there were 1,000 members of the Air Force in Mesopotamia, and that another sum of close upon £500,000 ought therefore to be shown in the account for Mesopotamia. We doubt this figure. We doubt all the Government figures. What about the cost of the new aerodromes, the sites of which are being selected by Sir John Salmond? But we will not pursue further the long series of evasions, of subterfuges, of concealments, and or positive misstatements, with which the whole of the Government's wild adventure in Mesopotamia is clouded.

There are two other points, however, which cannot be left unmentioned. Mr. Lloyd George had the temerity to allege that the late Lord Kitchener wanted us to place our outposts in the mountains of Northern Kurdistan. It is notorious that Lord Kitchener looked with horror and dismay upon the whole Mesopotamian adventure, and did his utmost to stop even the original advance upon Baghdad. The other point is that Mr. Lloyd George declared that Mr. Asquith wanted to accept responsibility for the whole of Mesopotamia and quoted the Sykes-Picot agreement as a proof. Clearly the Prime Minister is no more familiar with maps than with facts. The Sykes-Picot agreement only gave Great Britain a small area of territory as far as Baghdad; and as a matter of fact, the late Sir Mark Sykes had the most peremptory instructions from Mr. Asquith's Government, which he faithfully fulfilled, not to accept any direct responsibility within hundreds of miles of Mosul.

Mr. Lloyd George played his trump card when he

announced the scheme for setting up an Arab administration at Baghdad; but he gave no details, for he was not in possession of any. Details never trouble the Prime Minister when his back is to the wall and he has a case to make out. We will deal with the question of the Arab administration when we know what it amounts to. If the present heads of the civil administration in Mesopotamia remain there, we do not think the Arab will get much chance. But the real point is that, so far as we can gather from Mr. Lloyd George, the troops are to remain In Mesopotamia and on the road to the Caspian for an indefinite period, which means that their withdrawal will come at the Greek Kalends. The charge of £30.000.000 or £40,000,000 a year to the British taxpayer will therefore remain likewise. Mr. Lloyd George says: "Let us keep steady." We prefer to say what the whole nation is saying: "Let us keep solvent." Mr. Lloyd George says that what he proposes will add something to "the lustre of this great Empire." Nothing that he, of all men, can propose at this time of day will add to the lustre of thin old and proud race of Empire-builders; but there are no more tragic figures than the bankrupt heirs of great estates, ruined by megalomania.

Article From: THE MANCHESTER GUARDIAN
June 24, 1920

THE BRITISH MANDATE

After the meeting of the Supreme Council at San Remo, it was announced that the Mandate for Mesopotamia had been assigned to Greet Britain, and in the draft treaty presented to Turkey, it is provided (according to the official summary) that the boundaries of the Mesopotamian State, as well as the selection of the mandatory, shall be fixed by the principal Allied Powers. The terms of the mandates are likewise to be drafted by the principal Allied Powers, but are then to be submitted to the Council of the League of Nations for approval. Subject to these conditions, Mesopotamia is to be recognized provisionally by the high contracting parties to the treaty as an independent State, in accordance with article 22 of the Covenant of the League of Nations.

The mandate, then, for Mesopotamia is ours; we are to settle the boundaries by agreement with France and Italy; and even the terms of the mandate are to be drafted by ourselves and the other two principal Allies, and only submitted to the League for approval. The League is rather markedly thrust into the background, and this, whether we approve of it or regret it, makes our own responsibility the greater. Now at least, if not before, the question of Mesopotamia ought to be thoroughly debated in Parliament and in the press. Our administrative policy there will intimately affect our military and financial policy at home, and it ought not to be a matter of indifference to public opinion.

What are the chief points to consider? Let us clear the ground at once by saying that, so far as the defense of India is concerned, we could safely evacuate Mesopotamia to-morrow and withdraw to our pre-war positions in the Persian Gulf, as they were in 1914. In 1914, not merely the Mesopotamia hinter land of the Gulf, but an immense territory stretching from the Gulf to the Bosphorus, was under the sovereignty of the Ottoman Empire, a comparatively strong military power. Bin Saud, the most important Arabian ruler on the western littoral of the Gulf, was under Ottoman suzerainty; and behind the Ottoman Empire stood Germany, pushing her commercial and military penetration of Turkey nearer and nearer to Basra and Kuwait.

On the other flank, Persia, the Sovereign of the eastern littoral of the Gulf, was falling more and more under the ascendancy of Russia, and though the Anglo-Russian Agreement of 1907 kept Russian influence at a distance from the Gulf coast, the Central Government at Teheran seemed destined to come completely under Russia control. And yet our position in the Gulf was so strong that with the goodwill of our friends the Sheikh of Muhammerah and the Sheikh of Kuwait we were able to occupy Basra within a few weeks of Turkey's intervention in the war.

After that, our operations in Mesopotamia ceased to be measures for the defence of India and became an offensive movement against the military forces of Turkey and against the political domination of the Turks over an Arab population.

But if our position in the Gulf was so favorable in 1914, it has been infinitely strengthened by the break-up of the Ottoman, German, and Russian Empires, The German *Drang nach Osten,* has been dammed back behind the western frontiers of Szecho-Slovakia and Yugo-Slavia; the nearest Turkish troops and officials to the Gulf, instead of being at Basra, are now at Diarbekr, near the sources of the Tigris; and the British Empire has obtained a special political position in Persia, Central Arabia, and Mesopotamia, to the exclusion of other foreign powers, by treaties in the two former cases and by mandate in the latter.

In these circumstances it is impossible to contain that the defence of India requires the military occupation of a foot of Mesopotamia territory. Our position in the Gulf is not unlike Italy's in the Adriatic, and we are incredulous when the Italians argue that they need to hold more strategic positions in the Adriatic after the break-up of Austria-Hungary than before it. The dissolution of Italy's formidable neighbor in the Adriatic into half a dozen weak States cannot have so worsened Italy's strategic position that she needs additional security. This argument applies to us in the Gulf and with even more force, for our pre-war position there proved more than adequate for the conduct of war, while Italy's pre-war position in the Adriatic proved to be disadvantageous compared with Austria-Hungary's, though not with that of the Habsburg monarchy's divided heirs.

We can, therefore, simplify the Mesopotamian problem by eliminating considerations of Indian defence. Our pre-war naval and political position in the Gulf guarantees that. Our military policy in Mesopotamia can decide exclusively with reference to the country itself and to our home politics in Great Britain. At present we are maintaining an effective military occupation of the whole country, including Mosul. Under the mandate, is this to go on?

It is an urgent question, because Mesopotamia, within these limits, is one of the least defensible countries in the world. It is an open plain passing on one side into a desert inhabited by predatory Bedouin, and the other into a tangle of mountains inhabited by predatory Kurdish tribes - as difficult to keep in order as the tribesmen on the North-west frontier of India. A new North-west frontier, with an equally long and difficult desert frontier on the other side, is a military burden which we cannot lightly undertake, under the growing tensions in India and Egypt and after the exhaustion of the war. And it is evident that the burden would be enormously diminished if we drew in our outposts from the deserts and the foothills towards the center of the plain, where tanks, mechanical transport, and aeroplanes could be employed for defense to full advantage. Military experts have suggested that an area extending from the head of the Gulf to Kut-el-Amara could be defended with the minimum of effort. It would be covered by the course of the Tigris, the Shaztt-el-Hai marshes, and the marshes along the Euphrates below Nasiriyeh, and every hostile attack on it would have to be made across the open plain. This would leave us with a far more tolerable military burden in Mesopotamia than the burden we bear at present, but it must be repeated that even this restricted occupation is unnecessary for the defence of India, and that the military requirements, if any, of our mandates in Mesopotamia itself are all that have to be taken into account in this connection.

The issue between this restricted military occupation and the present occupation up to Mosul was raised in thee House of Commons on March 26. Mr. Asquith urged the former on the grounds of financial and military economy; Mr. Lloyd George argued in reply that the resources of the northern districts (e.g., the Mosul oilfields) would more than pay for the difference in the cost of defence, and hinted at the wider point that the area we now occupy is an economic and national unit, while Mr. Asquith's restricted area is not a possible unit either of the Mr. Asquith government or of irrigation. This has, of course, been our administrative experience since the occupation. Purely technical considerations have led to an increasing unification between the Basra, Bagdad, and Mosul districts in all departments.

But the Prime Minister's speech on this occasion cannot be the final word. Granting that the Mesopotamia plain, including Mosul, ought to be held together as one economy and political unit, that only settles the boundaries, and not the terms on which our mandate is to be exercised. Article 22 of the Covenant pledges us to render administrative advice and assistance to the people of Mesopotamia until such time as they are able to stand alone. Is the Prime Minister's policy of an effective military occupation of the country, paid for by exploitation of its natural resources, compatible with bold and rapid experiments in native self-government? Once foreign capital has been sunk in the oilfields the security of this investments might easily become the determining factor, and experiments in self-government might be hampered or even thwarted altogether by it. Moreover, Englishmen who have been administrating Mesopotamia since the occupation are full of warnings against any rapid exploitation of the resources of the country, an account of the administrative, social, and racial complications that, in their opinion, it would involve.

The right policy may therefore be one, which was not been discussed either by Mr. Asquith or by Mr. Lloyd George. It may be wisest to budget for no immediate economic returns from Mesopotamia such as would be needed to pay for an occupation up to Mosul, and to aim at evacuating Mesopotamia in the military sense altogether, retiring to our pre-war positions in the Persian Gulf. We cannot do this at once because we cannot leave the country without a government, but we might content ourselves with establishing a native Government of much lower efficiency than ours, and might then use our mandate in order to improve this native Government very gradually by the kind of influence, which we exercise upon the Native States of India. This policy at least deserves consideration as well as the other two.

Article From: THE SPECTATOR
June 18, 1921

Mr. Chruchill's eloquent and interesting speech on the Middle East in the House of Commons on Tuesday reminds us of a phenomenon familiar in the regions in which he was dealing. The weary traveler toiling over the stony desert sees in the distance an oasis, verdant and cool, with palm-trees that cast a grateful shade over a crystal spring. He takes an involuntary pleasure in the sight, contrasting so vividly with the barren wastes around him, but he knows that it is only a mirage – an optical illusion which will fade as he advances. It is in this spirit that we regard Mr. Churchill's oratorical enchantments. He summons up visions of an Arab State in Mesopotamia, managing its own affairs peacefully, while Southern Kurdistan enjoys Home Rule, and the nomad or semi-nomad tribes of Arabia from the Jordan to the Euphrates and the Persian Gulf accepting the supervision of the British Mandatory. Furthermore, he suggests that the cost of guiding the Arabs in the way in which they should go and of protecting them from external aggression is to diminish rapidly, and that the British garrisons may be withdrawn at a comparatively early date, leaving Arab forces trained by us to defend Arab liberties. The speech reads will, but our instinct warns us that it is based on theories and assumptions as intangible as the desert traveller's vision.

Mr. Churchill said that, having accepted a Mandate for Mesopotamia and Palestine, we could not light-heartedly repudiate our undertakings. We are, in effect, trustees for these regions, and we "must endeavour to do our duty in a sober and honourable manner." We may stress Mr. Churchill's admission that the obligation was not unlimited and that "a point might be reached when we should have to declare that we had failed and that we were not justified in demanding further sacrifices from the British taxpayer." He went on to say that, "if we were to avoid the shame of failure, the only key lay in the reduction of expenditure on these countries within reasonable and practicable limits." These are important conditions restricting the terrible responsibilities of the Mandates which the Government so thoughtlessly accepted, without stopping to count the cost. The question is whether Mr. Churchill's new project is likely to limit our commitments in Mesopotamia and to give that country a stable government. No one, not even Mr. Churchill himself, can confidently affirm that it will.

His plan is to hold Irak, from Basra to Baghdad and perhaps to Mosul, with a garrison of twelve British battalions, and eight air squadrons. All the Indian troops have been or are being sent home. An Arab army is being formed under a melodramatic hero named Jaafer Pasha, who fought for the Turks and against the Turks with equal zeal, and is now Secretary of War at Baghdad. There are also some Arab levies in our pay who have not yet earn much commendation. Provided that the river and desert tribes and the Kurds in the hills do not rise in insurrection, and provided that the Turks and the Bolsheviks from the north and Ibn Saud from the south do not invade Mesopotamia, this military provision may prove sufficient. Mr.

Churchill hopes to avert any fresh rising by setting up an Arab government. The people are to elect a National Assembly this summer, and the Assembly is to choose a ruler. Mr. Churchill's nominee for the post is the Emir Feisul, son of the King of the Kedj£az. Mr. Churchill admits that he does not know whether the people of Mesopotamia, who are rent with tribal, sectarian, racial, and economic feuds, will choose the Emir Feisul. If they do, Mr. Churchill thinks that they will make a wise decision. But here again, we are confronted with a mere hypothesis. It is well known that Ibn Saud, the head of the Wahhabis in South-eastern Arabia, whom Mr. Churchill described as the most militant Puritans of Islam, is an open enemy of the Kind of the Hedjaz and his family. Mr. Churchill thinks to curb his ambitions by a subsidy of £5,000 a month, paid on evidence of his good behaviour during each month, but Ibn Saud may not be able to restrain his fanatical followers. Mr. Churchill admits that the success of his whole plan ultimately depends upon the conclusion of peace with the Tucks who, through the ineptitude of the Allies, were given time to recover from utter defeat and are now almost as bellicose and impudent as ever. Thus when we analyse this attractive project we find that it consists almost entirely of assumptions which may be falsified. There is no real substance to it.

The Colonial Secretary's claims to have effected great economies are no more convincing. What we know is that the Middle East is going to cost us £27,500,000 this year. It is, of course, comforting to find that the original estimate of £35,000,000 has been reduced, but the comfort is illusory. When

Mr. Churchill talks of saving money, he reminds us of the lady who came home from a shopping expedition and told her husband that she saved ten guineas. It turned out, of course, that she had coveted a twenty-guinea had and that she had afterwards found a ten-guinea had which pleased her just as much. In buying the cheaper hat she appeared to save money, but the husband, stupid fellow, could not see it. All he knew was that he was ten guineas poorer. The Colonial Secretary, with all his clever explanations, cannot disguise the fact that the British taxpayer, who is at wit's end to know who to pay his Income Tax of six shillings in the pound, is contributing this year £27,250,000 towards the administration of Mesopotamia and Palestine, for he will get nothing – not even thanks – in return.

1. Egan, Eleanor Franklin, The War In The Cradle Of The World (London: Harper & Brothers Publishers, 1918)
1.1 Evans, R, *A Brief Outline Of The Campaign In Mesopotamia 1914-1918* (London: Sifton Praed & Co. Ltd. 1930)
2. Armstrong, Karen, *Islam: A Short History.* (New York: Modern Library. 2002) 30
3. Glubb John, *War in the Desert.* (New York: W.W. Norton and Company, Inc. 1960) 36
4. Glubb John, *War in the Desert,* 43
5. Armstrong, Karen, *Islam: A Short History,* 43
6. Lunt, James. *Imperial Sunset.* (London: Macdonald Futura Publishers. 1982) 21
7. Fischer, Fritz. *Germany's Aims in the First World War.* (New York: W. W. Norton and Company. 1967) 121
8. Hopkirk, Peter. *Like Hidden Fire: The Plot to Bring Down the British Empire.* (New York: Kodansha America, Inc. 1994) 28
9. Erickson, Edward. *Ordered to Die.* (Westport: Greenwood Press. 2001) 11
10. Fromkin, David. *A Peace to End All Peace.* (New York: Avon. 1989) 122
11. Yasamee, F. A. K. *Ottoman Empire. In Decisions for War, 1914.* Keith Wilson, ed., 229-268. (New York: St. Martin's Press. 1995) 259
12. Tuchman, Barbara. *The Guns of August.* (New York: Macmillan. 1962) 201
13. Tuchman, Barbara. *The Guns of August.* 164
14. Moberly, F. J. *The Campaign in Mesopotamia, 1914-1918. Vols. 1-4.* (London: H.M. Stationary Office. 1923) 1:58
15. Evans, R, *A Brief Outline Of The Campaign In Mesopotamia 1914-1918*
16. Jennings, Ivor. *Cabinet Government.* (London: Cambridge University Press. 1959) 296

17. 14. Moberly, F. J. *The Campaign in Mesopotamia, 1914-1918. Vols. 1-4.* 2:30
18. Beaumont, Roger. 1977. *Sword of the Raj.* (Indianapolis: The Bob-Merrill Company, Inc.) 156
19. Robertson, William. *Soldiers and Statesman, Vols. 1 and 2.* (Worcester: Billing and Sons, Ltd. 1991) 2:159
20. Moberly, F. J. *The Campaign in Mesopotamia, 1914-1918. Vols. 1-4.* 1:70
21. Moberly, F. J. *The Campaign in Mesopotamia, 1914-1918. Vols. 1-4.* 1:124
22. Moberly, F. J. *The Campaign in Mesopotamia, 1914-1918. Vols. 1-4.* 1:352
23. Moberly, F. J. *The Campaign in Mesopotamia, 1914-1918. Vols. 1-4.* 1:353
24. Hopkirk, Peter. *Like Hidden Fire: The Plot to Bring Down the British Empire.* 60
25. Keegan, John. *The First World War.* (New York: First Vintage Books. 2000) 218
26. Lt Staples, Letter quoted in *FM Lord Carver: The NAM Book of the Turkish Front, 1914-18.*
27. Robertson, William. *Soldiers and Statesman, Vols. 1 and 2.* 1:41
28. Maj Gen Melliss, letter quoted in *FM Lord Carver: The NAM Book of the Turkish Front, 1914-18.*
30. Maj Gen Melliss, letter quoted in *FM Lord Carver: The NAM Book of the Turkish Front, 1914-18.*
31. Lt H C West, RHA, quoted in *The Royal Artillery Commemoration Book.*
32. Maj Gen Melliss, letter quoted in *FM Lord Carver: The NAM Book of the Turkish Front, 1914-18.*
33. Maj Gen Sir Charles Townshend: *My Campaign in Mesopotamia.*

34. Maj Gen Melliss, letter quoted in *FM Lord Carver: The NAM Book of the Turkish Front, 1914-18.*
35. Moberly, F. J. *The Campaign in Mesopotamia, 1914-1918. Vols. 1-4.*
36. Moberly, F. J. *The Campaign in Mesopotamia, 1914-1918. Vols. 1-4.*
37. Robertson, William. *Soldiers and Statesman, Vols. 1 and 2.* 2:37-9
38. Robertson, William. *Soldiers and Statesman, Vols. 1 and 2.* 2:45-7
39. Barker, A. J. *The Bastard War.* (New York: The Dial Press. 1967) 95
40. Robertson, William. *Soldiers and Statesman, Vols. 1 and 2.* 2:42
41. Erickson, Edward. *Ordered to Die.* 112
42. Erickson, Edward. *Ordered to Die.* 112
43. Kearsey, A. *A Study of the Strategy and Tactics of the Mesopotamia Campaign.* (London: Gale and Polden, Ltd. 1934) 53
44. Erickson, Edward. *Ordered to Die.* 151
45. Keegan, John. *The First World War.* 300-1
46. Mesopotamia Commission. *Report of the Commission Appointed by Act of Parliament to Enquire into the Operations of War in Mesopotamia.* (London: H. M. Stationary Office. 1917) 103-7
47. Candler, Edmund. *The Long Road to Baghdad. Vols. 1 and 2.* (Boston and New York: Houghton Mifflin Company. 1919) 1:284
48. Candler, Edmund. *The Long Road to Baghdad. Vols. 1 and 2.* 1:288
49. Moberly, F. J. *The Campaign in Mesopotamia, 1914-1918. Vols. 1-4.* 1:110

50. Moberly, F. J. *The Campaign in Mesopotamia, 1914-1918. Vols. 1-4.* 2:398, 2:404
51. Mason, Philip. *A Matter of Honour.* (London: The Trinity Press. 1974) 442
52. Mason, Philip. *A Matter of Honour.* 443
53. Jennings, Ivor. *Cabinet Government.* 297
54. Evans, R, *A Brief Outline Of The Campaign In Mesopotamia 1914-1918*
54. Evans, R, *A Brief Outline Of The Campaign In Mesopotamia 1914-1918*
56. Robertson, William. *Soldiers and Statesman, Vols. 1 and 2.* 2:81
57. Moberly, F. J. *The Campaign in Mesopotamia, 1914-1918. Vols. 1-4.* 4:319
58. Moberly, F. J. *The Campaign in Mesopotamia, 1914-1918. Vols. 1-4.* 4:328
59. Robertson, William. *Soldiers and Statesman, Vols. 1 and 2.* 2:82
60. Robertson, William. *Soldiers and Statesman, Vols. 1 and 2.* 70
61. Candler, Edmund. *The Long Road to Baghdad. Vols. 1 and 2.* (Boston and New York: Houghton Mifflin Company. 1919) 1:109
62. Fromkin, David. *A Peace to End All Peace.* 192
63. Fromkin, David. *A Peace to End All Peace.* 375
64. Busch, Briton. *Britain, India, and the Arabs, 1914-21.* (Berkley: University of California Press. 1971) 71-8
65. Busch, Briton. *Britain, India, and the Arabs, 1914-21.* 199
66. Dodge, Toby. *Inventing Iraq.* (New York: Columbia University Press. 2003) 5-7
67. Omissi, David. *Air Power and Colonial Control.* (Manchester: Manchester University Press. 1990) 20
68. Yaphe, Judith. *The Challenge of Nation Building. In Decisions for War, 1914.* Keith Wilson, ed., 229-268. (New York: St. Martin's Press. 1995) 385

69. Busch, Briton. *Britain, India, and the Arabs, 1914-21.* 285
70. MacMillan, Margaret. *Paris, 1919.* (New York: Random House Trade Paperbacks. 2003) 397
71. Dodge, Toby. *Inventing Iraq.* 7
72. Busch, Briton. *Britain, India, and the Arabs, 1914-21.* 356
73. Wilson, Arnold. *Mesopotamia. 1917-1920: A Clash of Loyalties.* (London: Oxford University Press. 1931) 104
74. Busch, Briton. *Britain, India, and the Arabs, 1914-21.* 477-8
75. Tripp, Charles. 2000. *A History of Iraq.* Cambridge: Cambridge University Press. 33-4
76. Tripp, Charles. 2000. *A History of Iraq.* 40
77. Tripp, Charles. 2000. *A History of Iraq.* 39
78. Fromkin, David. *A Peace to End All Peace.* 377-8
79. MacMillan, Margaret. *Paris, 1919.* 392
80. MacMillan, Margaret. *Paris, 1919.* 384-5
81. MacMillan, Margaret. *Paris, 1919.* 405
82. Dodge, Toby. *Inventing Iraq.* 31
83. MacMillan, Margaret. *Paris, 1919.* 407
84. Tripp, Charles. 2000. *A History of Iraq.* 40
85. Tripp, Charles. 2000. *A History of Iraq.* 41
86. Tripp, Charles. 2000. *A History of Iraq.* 40
87. Tripp, Charles. 2000. *A History of Iraq.* 43
88. Marr, Phebe. *The Modern History of Iraq.* (Boulder: Westview Press. 1985) 33
89. Tripp, Charles. 2000. *A History of Iraq.* 40
90. Clayton, Anthony. *The British Empire as a Superpower, 1919-39.* (Athens: University of Georgia Press. 1986) 122
91. Yasamee, F. A. K. *Ottoman Empire. In Decisions for War, 1914.* 271
92. Clayton, Anthony. *The British Empire as a Superpower, 1919-39.* 120-4

93. Jacobsen, Mark. *Only by the Sword: British Counter-Insurgency in Iraq, 1920.* Small Wars & Insurgencies 2, no. 2 (August 1991). 348
94. Clayton, Anthony. *The British Empire as a Superpower, 1919-39.* 123
95. Jacobsen, Mark. *Only by the Sword: British Counter-Insurgency in Iraq, 1920.* 352
96. Tripp, Charles. 2000. *A History of Iraq.* 44
97. Busch, Briton. *Britain, India, and the Arabs, 1914-21.* 408-9
98. Tripp, Charles. 2000. *A History of Iraq.* 44
99. Marr, Phebe. *The Modern History of Iraq.* 33
100. Dodge, Toby. *Inventing Iraq.* 123
101. Tripp, Charles. 2000. *A History of Iraq.* 44
102. Jacobsen, Mark. *Only by the Sword: British Counter-Insurgency in Iraq, 1920.* 358-9
103. Omissi, David. *Air Power and Colonial Control.* (Manchester: Manchester University Press. 1990) 24
104. Omissi, David. *Air Power and Colonial Control.* (Manchester: Manchester University Press. 1990) 25-6
105. Busch, Briton. *Britain, India, and the Arabs, 1914-21.* 403
106. Marr, Phebe. *The Modern History of Iraq.* 34
107. Tripp, Charles. 2000. *A History of Iraq.* 45
108. Hemphill, Paul. *The Formation of the Iraqi Army, 1921-33. In The Integration of Modern Iraq.* In Abbas Kelidar, ed. 88-109. (New York: St. Martin's Press. 1979) 94
109. Tripp, Charles. 2000. *A History of Iraq.* 47-8
110. Marr, Phebe. *The Modern History of Iraq.* 36
111. Tripp, Charles. 2000. *A History of Iraq.* 48-50
112. Marr, Phebe. *The Modern History of Iraq.* 36
113. Tripp, Charles. 2000. *A History of Iraq.* 44
114. Tripp, Charles. 2000. *A History of Iraq.* 53
115. Marr, Phebe. *The Modern History of Iraq.* 38

116. Marr, Phebe. *The Modern History of Iraq.* 38
117. Dodge, Toby. *Inventing Iraq.* 23
118. Dodge, Toby. *Inventing Iraq.* 24
119. Dodge, Toby. *Inventing Iraq.* 25
120. Dodge, Toby. *Inventing Iraq.* 25
121. Dodge, Toby. *Inventing Iraq.* 25
122. Dodge, Toby. *Inventing Iraq.* 25
123. Tripp, Charles. 2000. *A History of Iraq.* 58
124. Tripp, Charles. 2000. *A History of Iraq.* 58
125. Marr, Phebe. *The Modern History of Iraq.* 39
126. Marr, Phebe. *The Modern History of Iraq.* 40
127. Hemphill, Paul. *The Formation of the Iraqi Army, 1921-33. In The Integration of Modern Iraq.* 89
128. Hemphill, Paul. *The Formation of the Iraqi Army, 1921-33. In The Integration of Modern Iraq.* 97-8
129. Omissi, David. *Air Power and Colonial Control.* 29
130. Omissi, David. *Air Power and Colonial Control.* 31
131. Hemphill, Paul. *The Formation of the Iraqi Army, 1921-33. In The Integration of Modern Iraq.* 95
132. Browne, Gilbert. The Iraq Levies, 1915-1932. (London: The Royal United Service Institution. 1932) 2-4
133. Browne, Gilbert. The Iraq Levies, 1915-1932. 4-5
134. Browne, Gilbert. The Iraq Levies, 1915-1932. 5
135. Lunt, James. *Imperial Sunset.* 31
136. Hemphill, Paul. *The Formation of the Iraqi Army, 1921-33. In The Integration of Modern Iraq.* 106
137. Browne, Gilbert. The Iraq Levies, 1915-1932. 13
138. Browne, Gilbert. The Iraq Levies, 1915-1932. 18-34
139. Lunt, James. *Imperial Sunset.* 35
140. Dodge, Toby. *Inventing Iraq.* 156
141. Dodge, Toby. *Inventing Iraq.* 131-3
142. Dodge, Toby. *Inventing Iraq.* 153-4

143. Towle, Philip. *Pilots and Rebels.* (London: Brassley's, Ltd. 1989) 22
144. Candler, Edmund. *The Long Road to Baghdad. Vols. 1 and 2.* 2:212-3
145. Barker, A. J. *The Bastard War.* 129-30
147. Hemphill, Paul. *The Formation of the Iraqi Army, 1921-33. In The Integration of Modern Iraq.* 94-5
148. Marr, Phebe. *The Modern History of Iraq.* 40
149. Marr, Phebe. *The Modern History of Iraq.* 41
150. Tripp, Charles. 2000. *A History of Iraq.* 54
151. Marr, Phebe. *The Modern History of Iraq.* 41
152. Tripp, Charles. 2000. *A History of Iraq.* 55
153. Marr, Phebe. *The Modern History of Iraq.* 41
154. Tripp, Charles. 2000. *A History of Iraq.* 59
155. Hemphill, Paul. *The Formation of the Iraqi Army, 1921-33. In The Integration of Modern Iraq.* 101
156. Dodge, Toby. *Inventing Iraq.* 73
157. Dodge, Toby. *Inventing Iraq.* 63
158. Dodge, Toby. *Inventing Iraq.* 10
159. Moberly, F. J. *The Campaign in Mesopotamia, 1914-1918. Vols. 1-4.*
160. Quoted in A J Barker: The Neglected War.
161. Wilson, Arnold. *Mesopotamia, 1914-1917: Loyalties.* 12
162. Wilson, Arnold. *Mesopotamia, 1914-1917: Loyalties.* 13
163. Wilson, Arnold. *Mesopotamia, 1914-1917: Loyalties.* 12-13, 65
164. Moberly, F. J. *The Campaign in Mesopotamia, 1914-1918. Vols. 1-4.* 3:254
165. Wilson, Arnold. *Mesopotamia, 1914-1917: Loyalties.* 65
166. Wilson, Arnold. *Mesopotamia, 1914-1917: Loyalties.* 13
167. Bell, Gertrude. *Review of the Civil Administration in Mesopotamia.* (London: H. M. Stationary Office. 1920) 5
168. Wilson, Arnold. *Mesopotamia, 1914-1917: Loyalties.* xi-xii

169. Gertrude Bell, D.B.E., *The Letters of Gertrude Bell, 2 vols.* (New York: Boni & Liveright. 1927) 2: 444
170. Gertrude Bell, D.B.E., *The Letters of Gertrude Bell, 2 vols.* 370, 378, 397-98
171. Wilson, Arnold. *Mesopotamia, 1914-1917: Loyalties.* 70
172. Bell, Gertrude. *Review of the Civil Administration in Mesopotamia.* 7
173. Bell, Gertrude. *Review of the Civil Administration in Mesopotamia.* 6
174. Wilson, Arnold. *Mesopotamia, 1914-1917: Loyalties.* 69-73, 289
175. Wilson, Arnold. *Mesopotamia, 1914-1917: Loyalties.* 283-87, 321-22
176. Wilson, Arnold. *Mesopotamia, 1914-1917: Loyalties.* 14
177. Bell, Gertrude. *Review of the Civil Administration in Mesopotamia.* 6
178. Maj Gen Sir Charles Townshend: *My Campaign in Mesopotamia.* 1: 226-27
179. Wilson, Arnold. *Mesopotamia, 1914-1917: Loyalties.* 12, 54
180. Moberly, F. J. *The Campaign in Mesopotamia, 1914-1918. Vols. 1-4.* 3:367
181. Wilson, Arnold. *Mesopotamia, 1914-1917: Loyalties.* 237-8
182. Busch, Briton. *Britain, India, and the Arabs, 1914-21.* 146
183. Wilson, Arnold. *Mesopotamia, 1914-1917: Loyalties.* 241
184. Candler, Edmund. *The Long Road to Baghdad. Vols. 1 and 2.* 2:119-120
186. Wilson, Arnold. *Mesopotamia, 1914-1917: Loyalties.* 241
187. Busch, Briton. *Britain, India, and the Arabs, 1914-21.* 147
188. Wilson, Arnold. *Mesopotamia, 1914-1917: Loyalties.* 240
189. Busch, Briton. *Britain, India, and the Arabs, 1914-21.* 149
190. Wilson, Arnold. *Mesopotamia, 1914-1917: Loyalties.* 240
191. Busch, Briton. *Britain, India, and the Arabs, 1914-21.* 148

192. Busch, Briton. *Britain, India, and the Arabs, 1914-21.* 151
193. Wilson, Arnold. *Mesopotamia, 1914-1917: Loyalties.* 242
194. Wilson, Arnold. *Mesopotamia, 1914-1917: Loyalties.* 21
195. Bell, Gertrude. *Review of the Civil Administration in Mesopotamia.* 49
196. Wilson, Arnold. *Mesopotamia. 1917-1920: A Clash of Loyalties.* 21
197. Marr, Phebe. *The Modern History of Iraq.* 31
198. Marr, Phebe. *The Modern History of Iraq.* 32
199. Bell, Gertrude. *Review of the Civil Administration in Mesopotamia.* 11
200. Wilson, Arnold. *Mesopotamia. 1917-1920: A Clash of Loyalties.* 173-4
201. Bell, Gertrude. *Review of the Civil Administration in Mesopotamia.* 12
202. Wilson, Arnold. *Mesopotamia. 1917-1920: A Clash of Loyalties.* 175-7
203. Wilson, Arnold. *Mesopotamia. 1917-1920: A Clash of Loyalties.* 175
204. Bell, Gertrude. *Review of the Civil Administration in Mesopotamia.* 11
205. Foster, Henry. *The Making of Modern Iraq.* (Norman: University of Oklahoma Press. 1935) 257
206. Hemphill, Paul. *The Formation of the Iraqi Army, 1921-33. In The Integration of Modern Iraq.* 92
207. Foster, Henry. *The Making of Modern Iraq.* 263
208. Foster, Henry. *The Making of Modern Iraq.* 263-4
210. Dodge, Toby. *Inventing Iraq.* 182
211. Glubb John, *War in the Desert,* 70-2
213. Dodge, Toby. *Inventing Iraq.* 84-5
214. Wilson, Arnold. *Mesopotamia, 1914-1917: Loyalties.* 67
215. Foster, Henry. *The Making of Modern Iraq.* 213

216. Foster, Henry. *The Making of Modern Iraq.* 214
217. Wilson, Arnold. *Mesopotamia, 1914-1917: Loyalties.* 68-9
218. Bell, Gertrude. *Review of the Civil Administration in Mesopotamia.* 101
219. Wilson, Arnold. *Mesopotamia. 1917-1920: A Clash of Loyalties.* 171-2
220. Dodge, Toby. *Inventing Iraq.* 92-3
221. Dodge, Toby. *Inventing Iraq.* 121-3
222. Dodge, Toby. *Inventing Iraq.* 94
223. Bell, Gertrude. *Review of the Civil Administration in Mesopotamia.* 15
224. Dodge, Toby. *Inventing Iraq.* 96
225. Wilson, Arnold. *Mesopotamia. 1917-1920: A Clash of Loyalties.* 172
226. Dodge, Toby. *Inventing Iraq.* 107
227. Tripp, Charles. 2000. *A History of Iraq.* 60
228. Al-Eyd, Kadhim. *Oil Revenues and Accelerated Growth.* (New York: Praeger Publishers. 1979) 13
229. Tripp, Charles. 2000. *A History of Iraq.* 60
230. Al-Eyd, Kadhim. *Oil Revenues and Accelerated Growth.* 14

## ADDITIONAL READING ON THE SUBJECT

Abbas Kelidar, ed. 1979. The Integration of Modern Iraq. New York: St. Martin's Press.

Amal Vinogradov,1972. The 1920 Revolt in Iraq Reconsidered: The Role of Tribes in National Politics. International Journal of Middle East Studies 3, no. 2 (April): 123-139.

British Official History, 2: 18; Great Britain, Parliament, Commissions, Mesopotamia Commission: Report of the Commission Appointed by Act of Parliament to Enquire into the Operations of War in Mesopotamia Together with a Separate Report by Cdr. J. Wedgwood, D.S.O., M.P. and Appendices (London: His Majesty's Stationery Office, 1917)

C. E. Callwell, 1990. Small Wars: A Tactical Textbook for Imperial Soldiers. London: Greenhill Books.

Charles Chenevix Trench, The Indian Army and the King's Enemies, 1900-1947. New York: Thames & Hudson, 1988.

Eleanor Franklin Egan, The War in the Cradle of the World. New York: Harper & Row, 1918.

F. W. Perry, The Commonwealth Armies: Manpower and

Organization in Two World Wars (Manchester, England: Manchester University Press, 1988)

FM Lord Carver: The NAM Book of the Turkish Front, 1914-18.

Hon. Sir Arthur Lawley, G.C.S.I., G.C.I.E., A Message from Mesopotamia (London: Hodder & Stoughton, 1917)

Lt. Col. A. H. Burne , D.S.O. Mesopotamia: The Last Phase. London: Gale & Polden, 1936.

Martin Swayne, In Mesopotamia (London: Hodder & Stoughton, 1918)

Paul K. Davis, Ends and Means: The British Mesopotamian Campaign and Commission (London: Associated University Presses)

Philip Mason, A Matter of Honour: An Account of the Indian Army, Its Officers, and Men (New York: Holt, Rinehart, and Winston, 1974)

Philip Mason, The Men Who Ruled India (New York: W. W. Norton & Co., 1985)

Russell Braddon, The Siege (New York, Viking Press, 1969).

Steven Metz, 2003-2004. Insurgency and Counterinsurgency in Iraq. The Washington Quarterly 27, no. 1 (winter): 25-36.

T. A. Heathcote, The Indian Army: The Garrison of Imperial India, 1822-1922, Historic Armies and Navies Series (New York: Hippocrene Books, 1974)

William Robertson, 1991. Soldiers and Statesman, Vols. 1 and 2. Worcester: Billing and Sons, Ltd.

'he Mesopotamia Mess

BN: 978-1-60299-017-3

**Order Form**

| Item No. / ISBN No. | Product Name | QTY | Price | Subtotal |
|---|---|---|---|---|
| 978-1-60299-017-3 | The Mesopotamia Mess | | $14.99 | |
| | | | Tax* | $ |
| | | | Shipping** | $ |
| :alifornia residents please add 8.25% sales tax<br>i% of subtotal with a $6 minimum | | | Total | $ |

me:________________________________________

mpany:______________________________________

dress:_______________________________________

_____________________________________________

ɔne: ____________________ Fax: ____________________

nail: ______________________________

·dit card purchases: ❑ Visa ❑ MasterCard ❑ American Express

·d # ______________________________Exp.____________

ne on card___________________________

423 South Pacific Coast Hwy., #208, Redondo Beach CA 90277
TheMesopotamiaMess@gmail.com • Tel: 310.792.3635 • Fax: 310.792.3642

Made in the USA